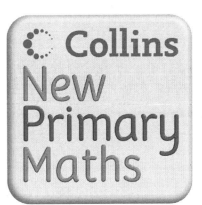

Speaking and Listening 3

Developing children's listening skills
in the daily maths lesson

Peter Clarke

William Collins' dream of knowledge for all began with the publication of his first book in 1819. A self-educated mill worker, he not only enriched millions of lives, but also founded a flourishing publishing house. Today, staying true to this spirit, Collins books are packed with inspiration, innovation and practical expertise. They place you at the centre of a world of possibility and give you exactly what you need to explore it.

Collins. Freedom to teach.

Published by Collins
An imprint of HarperCollins*Publishers* Ltd.
77-85 Fulham Palace Road
Hammersmith
London
W6 8JB

Browse the complete Collins catalogue at
www.collinseducation.com

© HarperCollins*Publishers* Ltd 2009

10 9 8 7 6 5 4 3 2 1

ISBN: 978-0-00-732281-7

Peter Clarke asserts his moral right to be identified as the author of this work.

British Library Cataloguing in Publication Data
A Catalogue record for this publication is available from the British Library.

Cover template: Laing&Carroll
Cover illustration: Jonatronix Ltd.
Series design: Neil Adams
Illustrations: Bethan Matthews, Jeffrey Reid, Lisa Williams, Mel Sharp, Rhiannon Powell, Tim Archbold, Roy Mitchell

Acknowledgement
The author wishes to thank Brian Molyneaux for his valuable contribution to this publication.

Printed and bound by Hobbs the Printers, UK

Mixed Sources
Product group from well-managed
forests and other controlled sources
www.fsc.org Cert no. SW-COC-1806
© 1996 Forest Stewardship Council

FSC is a non-profit international organisation established to promote the responsible management of the world's forests. Products carrying the FSC label are independently certified to assure consumers that they come from forests that are managed to meet the social, economic and ecological needs of present and future generations.

Find out more about HarperCollins and the environment at
www.harpercollins.co.uk/green

Contents

Introduction   4

Listening and communicating   4

Communication and mental imagery   4

The skills of listening   5

Becoming a good listener   5

Characteristics of a good listener   5

Collins New Primary Maths: Speaking and Listening and the
teaching–learning cycle   7

Curriculum information   7

Planning a programme of work for *Collins New Primary Maths:
Speaking and Listening*   7

Collins New Primary Maths: Speaking and Listening and the
daily mathematics lesson   7

Collins New Primary Maths: Speaking and Listening objectives coverage   8

Collins New Primary Maths: Speaking and Listening programme   9

How to use *Collins New Primary Maths: Speaking and Listening*   10

Collins New Primary Maths: Speaking and Listening and assessment   10

Collins New Primary Maths: Speaking and Listening assessment sheet   11

The activities   12

Strand 1: Using and applying mathematics   12

Strand 2: Counting and understanding number   16

Strand 3: Knowing and using number facts   26

Strand 4: Calculating   36

Strand 5: Understanding shape   58

Strand 6: Measuring   62

Strand 7: Handling data   70

Introduction

Collins New Primary Maths: Speaking and Listening is a series of seven books from Foundation to Year 6 which is designed to assist children in practising and consolidating objectives from the *Renewed Primary Framework for Mathematics* (2006) at the same time as developing their listening skills.

Listening and following instructions are two key skills that are crucial to the success of every child and every adult. How many times have children had to redo work because they have not listened to your directions? How many times do you have to repeat yourself? How often have you wished you could take time out from the overburdened curriculum to help children develop their listening skills? This series will help you solve these problems. You will not have to take time away from other curriculum areas to do this since *Collins New Primary Maths: Speaking and Listening* helps to develop children's listening skills and ability to follow oral directions while they practise valuable mathematical skills.

Listening and communicating

The purpose of this book is the development of children's listening skills through the mathematics curriculum, but this skill is not seen in isolation. Many of the activities outlined include reading, speaking and writing. Listening is an integral part of communication which deals with the process of giving and receiving information. The four different aspects of the communication process outlined below rely upon each other for effective communication at the same time as actively supporting and enriching one another.

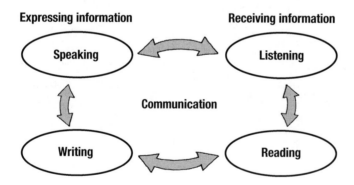

Communication and mental imagery

All children, whatever their age and ability, have their own mental images, developed from previous knowledge and experiences. Aural stimulus enables children to manipulate the mental images they have of numbers, shapes and measures. Instant recall of number facts such as the multiplication tables and the addition and subtraction number facts often depends on an aural input. Children have to hear the sounds in order to give an automatic response.

The difficult part for the teacher is to discover what is going on inside children's heads. This is where discussion as an accompaniment to mental work is so important. It is only through discussion that the teacher can begin to develop an insight into children's mental processes. Discussions also enable children to develop their own insights into their mental imagery and provide the opportunity for them to share their ideas and methods. They can form judgements about the alternatives, decide which methods are the most efficient and effective for them, and further develop flexibility and familiarity with the different mathematical topics.

The skills of listening

Listening skills can be improved through training and practice. When direct attention is paid to listening for specific purposes, and these skills are practised and consolidated, improvement in ability follows. In general children tend to learn and remember more through listening than in almost any other way. A high percentage of all the information children receive comes through their ears. Thus direct training in the skills of listening can be hugely beneficial to all learning.

Effective listening involves:
- hearing
- concentrating
- a knowledge of language
- a knowledge of the structure of language
- recognising cues
- being able to contextualise
- inferring
- thinking
- processing
- summarising
- selecting
- organising
- drawing upon previous knowledge and experience
- comprehending/understanding the main idea.

Becoming a good listener

Display the poster on page 6 to remind children of how to become a good listener. When concentrating on developing children's listening skills draw attention to the poster.

Characteristics of a good listener

A good listener is one who:
- knows how to listen
- is able to concentrate on listening
- looks at the speaker
- is courteous to the speaker
- does not interrupt the speaker
- is able to zero in on the speaker and eliminate extraneous noises and interruptions
- can comprehend
- is selective
- asks him/herself questions while listening
- draws upon their previous knowledge and experiences
- evaluates while listening
- remembers what is said
- anticipates what is coming next.

Good listening

Sit still

Think about the words

Look at the speaker

Collins New Primary Maths: Speaking and Listening 3 © HarperCollins*Publishers* Ltd 2009

Collins New Primary Maths: Speaking and Listening and the teaching–learning cycle

Assessment
- Each activity can be used to assess a specific objective from the *Renewed Primary Framework for Mathematics* (2006).
- Guidance given on how to record pupil performance.

Planning
- Each activity linked to an objective in the *Renewed Primary Framework for Mathematics* (2006)
- Guidance given for planning a programme of work.

Teaching
- Clear and complete instructions given for each activity.
- Ideally suited to the daily mathematics lesson.

Curriculum information

Each of the 30 activities is organised under specific objectives as identified in the *Renewed Primary Framework for Mathematics* (2006). The *Collins New Primary Maths: Speaking and Listening* objectives coverage chart on page 8 shows which activity is matched to which objective(s).

Planning a programme of work for *Collins New Primary Maths: Speaking and Listening*

The *Collins New Primary Maths: Speaking and Listening* programme chart on page 9 may be used in conjunction with your long- and medium-term plans to develop a *Collins New Primary Maths: Speaking and Listening* programme of work throughout the year. By following the Blocks and Units from the *Renewed Primary Framework for Mathematics* (2006) you will ensure that the children have the opportunity to practise and consolidate the strands, and specific objectives for a particular unit of work, at the same time as developing their listening skills.

Collins New Primary Maths: Speaking and Listening and the daily mathematics lesson

The activities contained in *Collins New Primary Maths: Speaking and Listening* are ideally suited to the daily mathematics lesson. Each activity is designed to be presented to the whole class. The activities are extremely flexible and can be used in a variety of ways. For example, activities can be used during the:
- oral work and mental calculation session to practise and consolidate previously taught concepts;
- main teaching part of the lesson to focus on particular skills and concepts;
- plenary session to consolidate the concept(s) taught during the main part of the lesson and to conclude the lesson in an enjoyable way.

Collins New Primary Maths: Speaking and Listening objectives coverage

STRAND	OBJECTIVES	ACTIVITY	PAGE
1: Using and applying mathematics	Solve one-step and two-step problems involving numbers, choosing and carrying out appropriate calculations. Describe and explain methods.	1	12
	Solve one-step and two-step problems involving money, choosing and carrying out appropriate calculations. Describe and explain methods.	2	14
2: Counting and understanding number	Count on from and back to zero in single-digit steps or multiples of 10.	3	16
	Read and write whole numbers to at least 1000. **Partition three-digit numbers into multiples of 100, 10 and 1 in different ways.**	4	18
	(Compare and) order whole numbers to at least 1000, (say which is more or less, and give a number which lies between them). (Say the number that is 1, 10 or 100 more or less than any given number to at least 1000).	5	20
	Round two-digit or three-digit numbers to the nearest 10 or 100.	6	22
	Read and write proper fractions, e.g. $\frac{3}{7}$, $\frac{9}{10}$, interpreting the denominator as the parts of a whole and the numerator as the number of parts.	7	24
3: Knowing and using number facts	**Derive and recall all addition and subtraction facts for each number to 20.**	8	26
	Derive and recall multiplication facts for the 2, 3, 4, 5 and 10 times-tables and the corresponding division facts.	9	28
	Derive and recall division facts corresponding to the 2, 5 and 10 times-tables.	10	30
	Recognise multiples of 2, 5 or 10 up to 1000 (and three-digit multiples of 50 and 100).	11	32
	Use knowledge of number operations and corresponding inverses, including doubling and halving. (Derive and recall doubles of whole numbers to at least 20, multiples of 5 to 100, multiples of 50 to 500, and the corresponding halves.)	12	34
4: Calculating	**Add mentally combinations of one-digit, two-digit** (and three-digit numbers and multiples of 10 and 100).	13	36
	Subtract mentally combinations of one-digit, two-digit (and three-digit numbers and multiples of 10 and 100).	14	38
	Add or subtract mentally combinations of one-digit, two-digit (and three-digit numbers and multiples of 10 and 100).	15	40
	Add or subtract mentally combinations of one-digit, two-digit (and three-digit numbers and multiples of 10 and 100).	16	42
	Develop and use written methods to record, support or explain addition of two-digit and three-digit numbers.	17	44
	Develop and use written methods to record, support or explain subtraction of two-digit and three-digit numbers.	18	46
	Develop and use written methods to record, support or explain addition and subtraction of two-digit and three-digit numbers.	19	48
	Use practical and informal written methods to multiply two-digit numbers.	20	50
	Use practical and informal written methods to divide two-digit numbers. (Divide multiples of 10 and 100 by 2, 10 or 100.)	21	52
	Use practical and informal written methods to multiply and divide two-digit numbers. Multiply one-digit and two-digit numbers by 10 or 100, and describe the effect. (Divide multiples of 10 and 100 by 2, 10 or 100.)	22	54
	Find unit fractions of numbers and quantities, e.g. $\frac{1}{2}$, $\frac{1}{3}$, $\frac{1}{4}$ and $\frac{1}{6}$ of 12 litres.	23	56
5: Understanding shape	Relate 2-D shapes and 3-D solids to drawings of them; describe, visualise, classify the shapes.	24	58
	Read and record the vocabulary of position, direction and movement.	25	60
6: Measuring	Solve one-step and two-step problems involving measures (length). **Read, to the nearest division and half-division, scales that are numbered or partially numbered.**	26	62
	Solve one-step and two-step problems involving measures (mass). **Read, to the nearest division and half-division, scales that are numbered or partially numbered.**	27	64
	Solve one-step and two-step problems involving measures (capacity). **Read, to the nearest division and half-division, scales that are numbered or partially numbered.**	28	66
	Read the time on a 12-hour digital clock and to the nearest five minutes on an analogue clock.	29	68
7: Handling data	Answer a question by collecting, organising and interpreting data; use tally charts, frequency tables, and bar charts to represent results and illustrate observations.	30	70

Key objectives are in bold.

Collins New Primary Maths: Speaking and Listening programme

YEAR
CLASS
TEACHER

	UNIT	MATHEMATICS STRANDS	CNPM: SPEAKING AND LISTENING ACTIVITY
AUTUMN	A1	**Counting, partitioning and calculating** Strand 1: Using and applying mathematics Strand 2: Counting and understanding number Strand 3: Knowing and using number facts Strand 4: Calculating	
	B1	**Securing number facts, understanding shapes** Strand 1: Using and applying mathematics Strand 3: Knowing and using number facts Strand 5: Understanding shape	
	C1	**Handling data and measures** Strand 1: Using and applying mathematics Strand 6: Measuring Strand 7: Handling data	
	D1	**Calculating, measuring and understanding shape** Strand 1: Using and applying mathematics Strand 4: Calculating Strand 5: Understanding shape Strand 6: Measuring	
	E1	**Securing number facts, calculating, identifying relationships** Strand 1: Using and applying mathematics Strand 2: Counting and understanding number Strand 3: Knowing and using number facts Strand 4: Calculating	
SPRING	A2	**Counting, partitioning and calculating** Strand 1: Using and applying mathematics Strand 2: Counting and understanding number Strand 3: Knowing and using number facts Strand 4: Calculating	
	B2	**Securing number facts, understanding shapes** Strand 1: Using and applying mathematics Strand 3: Knowing and using number facts Strand 5: Understanding shape	
	C2	**Handling data and measures** Strand 1: Using and applying mathematics Strand 6: Measuring Strand 7: Handling data	
	D2	**Calculating, measuring and understanding shape** Strand 1: Using and applying mathematics Strand 4: Calculating Strand 5: Understanding shape Strand 6: Measuring	
	E2	**Securing number facts, calculating, identifying relationships** Strand 1: Using and applying mathematics Strand 2: Counting and understanding number Strand 3: Knowing and using number facts Strand 4: Calculating	
SUMMER	A3	**Counting, partitioning and calculating** Strand 1: Using and applying mathematics Strand 2: Counting and understanding number Strand 3: Knowing and using number facts Strand 4: Calculating	
	B3	**Securing number facts, understanding shapes** Strand 1: Using and applying mathematics Strand 3: Knowing and using number facts Strand 5: Understanding shape	
	C3	**Handling data and measures** Strand 1: Using and applying mathematics Strand 6: Measuring Strand 7: Handling data	
	D3	**Calculating, measuring and understanding shape** Strand 1: Using and applying mathematics Strand 4: Calculating Strand 5: Understanding shape Strand 6: Measuring	
	E3	**Securing number facts, calculating, identifying relationships** Strand 1: Using and applying mathematics Strand 2: Counting and understanding number Strand 3: Knowing and using number facts Strand 4: Calculating	

How to use *Collins New Primary Maths: Speaking and Listening*

Preparation

■ Provide each child with the necessary resources. These can be found at the beginning of each activity's teacher's page.

Instructions

Explain the following to the children:

■ They need to listen carefully.

■ They will be given some oral instructions to follow.

■ The instructions will only be given once.

■ They must only do what they are told to do, nothing more.

■ They may not use an eraser.

■ How many instructions there are for the particular activity.

■ That they are to do each task immediately after the instructions for that part have been given.

The activity

■ If necessary, briefly discuss the pupil sheet with the children. Ensure that the children are familiar with the pictures and/or the text on the sheet.

■ Ensure that the children are also familiar with any of the terms used in the oral instructions. Refer to the *Key words* for a list of the relevant vocabulary.

■ Ask the children to write the date on the sheet in the space provided.

■ Do not ask the children to write their name. This will occur during the activity.

■ Slowly read the instructions to the children.

Discussion

■ After the children have completed the sheet, discuss the activity with the class. You may decide to do this either before or after marking the activity. Use the *Discussion questions* as a springboard. For each activity there are questions that have been designed to cater for higher attaining (↑) and lower attaining (↓) pupils.

Marking

■ Mark the sheet with the whole class, either before or after the discussion. You may wish the children to mark their own sheet or to swap with someone next to them. However, if you are using the activity as an assessment tool then you may decide to mark the sheets yourself at a later stage.

Revisiting an activity

■ Repeat an activity with the class at a later stage in the year. Children can compare how they performed on the task the second time round.

■ You may like to alter the activity slightly by changing one or two of the instructions.

Collins New Primary Maths: Speaking and Listening and assessment

Collins New Primary Maths: Speaking and Listening activities may be used with the whole class or with groups of children as an assessment activity. Linked to the topic that is being studied at present, *Collins New Primary Maths: Speaking and Listening* will provide you with an indication of how well the children have understood the objectives being covered as well as how their listening skills are developing. The *Collins New Primary Maths: Speaking and Listening* assessment sheet on page 11 may be used to record how well the children have understood the objectives covered in the activity.

Collins New Primary Maths: Speaking and Listening assessment sheet

YEAR
CLASS
TEACHER

/ Not understood   ∠ Developing an understanding   △ Completely understood

NAME	ACTIVITY																													
	1	2	3	4	5	6	7	8	9	10	11	12	13	14	15	16	17	18	19	20	21	22	23	24	25	26	27	28	29	30

Activity 1

Year 3 Using and applying mathematics

- Solve one-step and two-step problems involving numbers, choosing and carrying out appropriate calculations.
- Describe and explain methods.

Resources

Provide each child with the following:
- a copy of Activity 1 pupil sheet
- a pencil

Key words

zero, one, two...one hundred   left   added   one quarter
three quarters   shared evenly

Say to the children:

Listen carefully.

I am going to tell you some things to do.

I will say them only once, so listen very carefully.

Do only the things you are told to do and nothing else.

If you make a mistake, cross it out. Do not use an eraser.

There are 13 parts to this activity.

The activity

1. Look at the tray of chocolates. How many chocolates are on the tray? Write that number on box one.

2. How many chocolates would be left if 11 were eaten? Write that number on box six.

3. Look at the chocolates on the tray again. How many people could have four chocolates each? Write that number on box eight.

4. How many chocolates would there be if you had three trays? Write that number on box four.

5. If another nine chocolates were added to the tray how many chocolates would be on the tray? Write that number on box seven.

6. There are three different types of chocolates on the table. 15 are white chocolate. 10 are dark chocolate. How many are milk chocolate? Write that number on box eleven.

7. If one quarter of the chocolates were eaten how many would be left? Write that number on box nine.

8. How many trays would be needed to hold 64 chocolates? Write that number on box three.

9. Look at all the chocolate boxes around the tray. How many more chocolates would be needed if all the boxes were to have three chocolates in them? Write that number on box two.

10. Originally there were 45 chocolates on the tray. How many chocolates have been eaten? Write that number on box twelve.

11. How many trays would be needed to hold 80 chocolates? Write that number on box ten.

12. If three quarters of the chocolates on this tray were eaten, how many would be left? Write that number on box five.

13. Write your name at the top of the sheet.

Answers

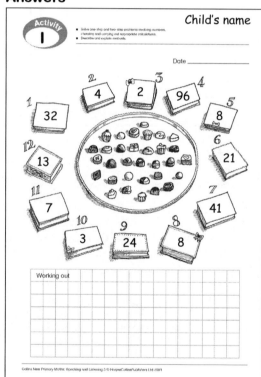

Discussion questions

↓ What number did you write on box one? (32)

↓ How many more chocolates would you need to add to the tray to make forty? (8)

■ What number did you write on box three? (2)

■ How many chocolates would there be on three trays? (96) Where did you write that answer? (box four)

↑ How many trays are needed to hold 80 chocolates? (3) Why?

↑ Look at all the chocolate boxes around the tray. How many more chocolates would be needed if all the boxes were to have three chocolates in them? (4) How did you work it out?

- Solve one-step and two-step problems involving numbers, choosing and carrying out appropriate calculations.
- Describe and explain methods.

Date _____

Working out												

- Solve one-step and two-step problems involving money, choosing and carrying out appropriate calculations.
- Describe and explain methods.

Resources

Provide each child with the following:
- a copy of Activity 2 pupil sheet
- a coloured pencil

Key words

coin money pence pound note change item most expensive

Say to the children:

Listen carefully.

I am going to tell you some things to do.

I will say them only once, so listen very carefully.

Do only the things you are told to do and nothing else.

If you make a mistake, cross it out. Do not use an eraser.

There are 13 parts to this activity.

The activity

On this sheet, if the answer to the question is yes, draw a ring around the picture. If the answer to the question is no, draw a cross through the picture. Use the jotting pad for any working out you might want to do.

1. Look at the packet of pencils. Josh has two one pound coins and a five pence coin. Does he have enough money to buy the packet of pencils?

2. Look at the baseball cap. Marcus has two one pound coins, two fifty pence coins, two twenty pence coins and a five pence coin. Does he have enough money to buy the baseball cap?

3. Look at the camera. Can Isabelle buy the camera if she has a five pound note, a fifty pence coin, a ten pence coin and a five pence coin?

4. Look at the box of chocolates. Can Catherine buy the box of chocolates if she has one two pound coin, three fifty pence coins, a twenty pence coin and a ten pence coin?

5. Look at the book. If Jean has a two pound coin, two one pound coins and a fifty pence coin, can she buy the book?

6. Look at the bus ticket. Mr and Mrs Dakin have ten pounds. They want to take the bus with their two children. Do they have enough money to take the bus together?

7. Look at the ice cream. Alison has three pounds. She wants to buy herself and two friends an ice cream each. Does she have enough money?

8. Look at the bunch of grapes. Mrs Zahar gave the grocer a two pound coin. She received back in change a fifty pence coin, two twenty pence coins and a two pence coin. Did Mrs Zahar receive the correct amount of change?

9. Look at the board game. Sarah has two two pound coins, a fifty pence coin, a twenty pence coin and a five pence coin. Does she have enough money to buy the board game?

10. Look at the light bulb. Can Brian buy the light bulb if he has a one pound coin, two fifty pence coins, and three two pence coins?

11. Look at the comic. Sam empties his money jar and finds that he has fifteen five pence coins. Does he have enough money to buy the comic?

12. Look at the roses. Tim has five pounds. Does he have enough money to buy six roses?

13. Look at all the items on the sheet. Write your name under the least expensive item.

Answers

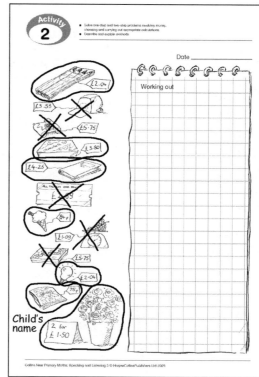

Discussion questions

↓ How many answers were 'yes'? (7)

↓ Which are the most expensive items on the sheet? (camera and board game)

■ Jean had £4.50. Did she have enough money to buy the book? (yes) How much change should Jean have received? (25p)

■ What is the smallest number of coins needed to buy the pencils? (3) What are they? (£2, 2p, 2p)

↑ How much was the bunch of grapes? (£1.09) Mrs Zahar gave the grocer a two pound coin. How much change should she have received? (91p)

↑ How much does one rose cost? (75p) How much would it cost for five/eight roses? (£3.75/£6)

■ Solve one-step and two-step problems involving money,
   choosing and carrying out appropriate calculations.
■ Describe and explain methods.

Date _____

£2.04

£3.55

£5.75

chocolate £3.80

£4.25

ALL TICKETS ONE PRICE
£2.99

84p

£1.09

£5.75

£2.04

75p

2 for £1.50

Working out

■ Count on from and back to zero in single-digit steps or multiples of 10.

Resources

Provide each child with the following:
■ a copy of Activity 3 pupil sheet
■ a red, blue, green, yellow, orange and purple coloured pencil

Key words

zero, one, two…one hundred   next

Say to the children:

Listen carefully.

I am going to tell you some things to do.

I will say them only once, so listen very carefully.

Do only the things you are told to do and nothing else.

If you make a mistake, cross it out. Do not use an eraser.

There are 13 parts to this activity.

The activity

1. Listen carefully as I count. 615, 515, 415, 315. What number comes next? Find that number and colour the bubble red.

2. 80, 75, 70, 65, 60. What number comes next? Find that number and colour the bubble red.

3. 52, 54, 56, 58. What number comes next? Find that number and colour the bubble blue.

4. 29, 26, 23, 20. What number comes next? Find that number and colour the bubble blue.

5. 500, 600, 700, 800. What number comes next? Find that number and colour the bubble green.

6. 10, 15, 20, 25, 30. What number comes next? Find that number and colour the bubble green.

7. 74, 72, 70, 68. What number comes next? Find that number and colour the bubble yellow.

8. 33, 43, 53, 63. What number comes next? Find that number and colour the bubble yellow.

9. 50, 46, 42, 38, 34. What number comes next? Find that number and colour the bubble orange.

10. 12, 15, 18, 21. What number comes next? Find that number and colour the bubble orange.

11. 51, 41, 31, 21. What number comes next? Find that number and colour the bubble purple.

12. 26, 30, 34, 38. What number comes next? Find that number and colour the bubble purple.

13. Write your name on the bottom of the lava lamp.

Answers

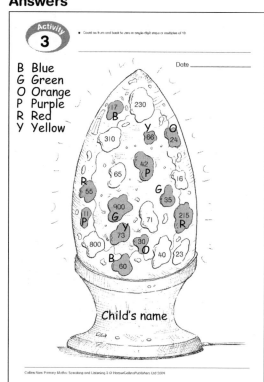

B Blue
G Green
O Orange
P Purple
R Red
Y Yellow

Discussion questions

↓ Which numbers did you colour blue? (60 and 17)

↓ Tell me a number you did not colour. (16, 23, 40, 65, 71, 230, 310, 800)

■ Start at 15 and count on in fours. (15, 19, 23, 27…)

■ Choose a number from the sheet and put it in a number sequence. What is the next number? What is the rule?

↑ If you start at 31 and count back in threes, what will be the fifth number in the sequence? (19)

↑ What are the two numbers you coloured orange? (30 and 24) Put these two numbers into a number sequence. (e.g. 24, 27, 30, 33, 36…)

■ Count on from and back to zero in single-digit steps or multiples of 10.

Date _____

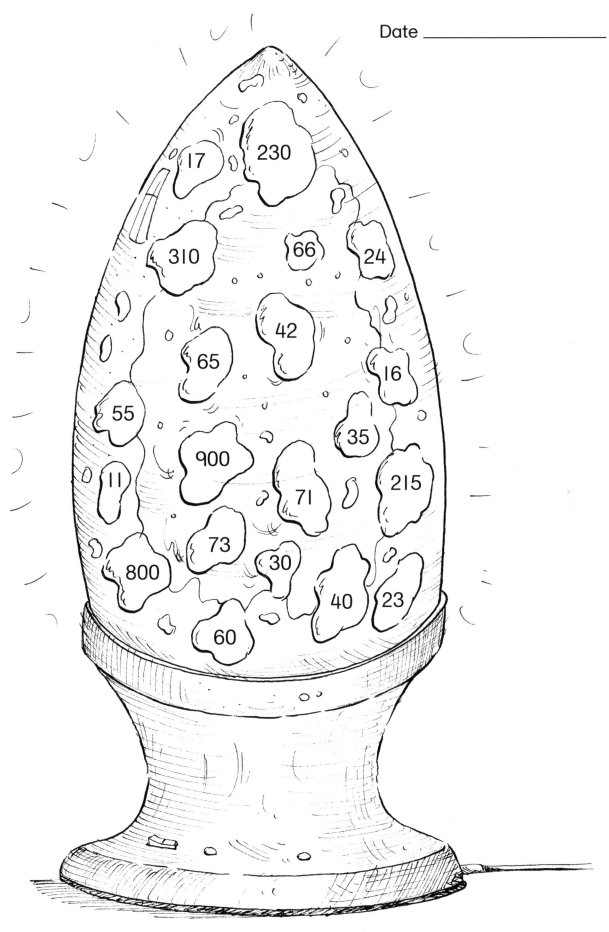

Activity 4

Year 3 Counting and understanding number

- Read and write whole numbers to at least 1000.
- Partition three-digit numbers into multiples of 100, 10 and 1 in different ways.

Resources

Provide each child with the following:
- a copy of Activity 4 pupil sheet
- a pencil
- a coloured pencil

Key words

zero, one, two…one thousand   abacus   digit   units/ones   tens   hundreds   represents   equivalent to   partition   multiple

Say to the children:

Listen carefully.

I am going to tell you some things to do.

I will say them only once, so listen very carefully.

Do only the things you are told to do and nothing else.

If you make a mistake, cross it out. Do not use an eraser.

There are 13 parts to this activity.

The activity

1. Look at abacus one. What number is the abacus showing? Write that number in the box underneath the abacus.

2. Look at abacus two. What number is this abacus showing? Write that number in the box underneath the abacus.

3. Look at abacus three. What number is this abacus showing? Write that number in the box underneath the abacus.

4. Look at the number underneath abacus four. Show this number on the abacus.

5. Look at the number underneath abacus five. Show this number on the abacus.

6. Look at the number underneath abacus six. Show this number on the abacus.

7. Look at abacus seven. Write the number 683 in the box underneath the abacus and then show this number on the abacus.

8. Look at abacus eight. Write the number 860 in the box underneath the abacus and then show this number on the abacus.

9. Look at abacus nine. Write the number 972 in the box underneath the abacus and then show this number on the abacus.

10. Write your name under the smallest number on the sheet.

11. Look at all the numbers on the sheet again. Which number is equivalent to 700 plus five tens plus eight units? Colour that number.

12. Again, look at all the numbers on the sheet. Which number has a one in the tens place? Colour that number.

13. Look at the two numbers you have just coloured. Write both of these numbers as words on the lines at the bottom of the sheet.

Answers

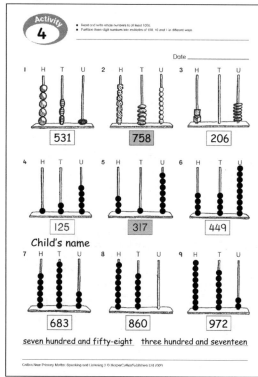

Discussion questions

↓ Which two numbers did you colour? (758 and 317)

↓ What is the smallest/largest number on the sheet? (125/972)

■ Which number has the same number of tens and hundreds? (449)

■ Which number has the largest digit in the tens place? (683)

↑ Listen carefully. Four hundreds, three units and nine tens. What number is this? (493) Can you write this number as a figure/word? (493/four hundred and ninety-three)

↑ Listen carefully. Seven hundreds plus no tens and five ones. What number is this? (705) How many units/tens/hundreds are there in this number? (5/0/7) Can you write this number as a figure/word? (705/seven hundred and five)

■ Read and write whole numbers to at least 1000.
■ Partition three-digit numbers into multiples of 100, 10 and 1 in different ways.

Date _____

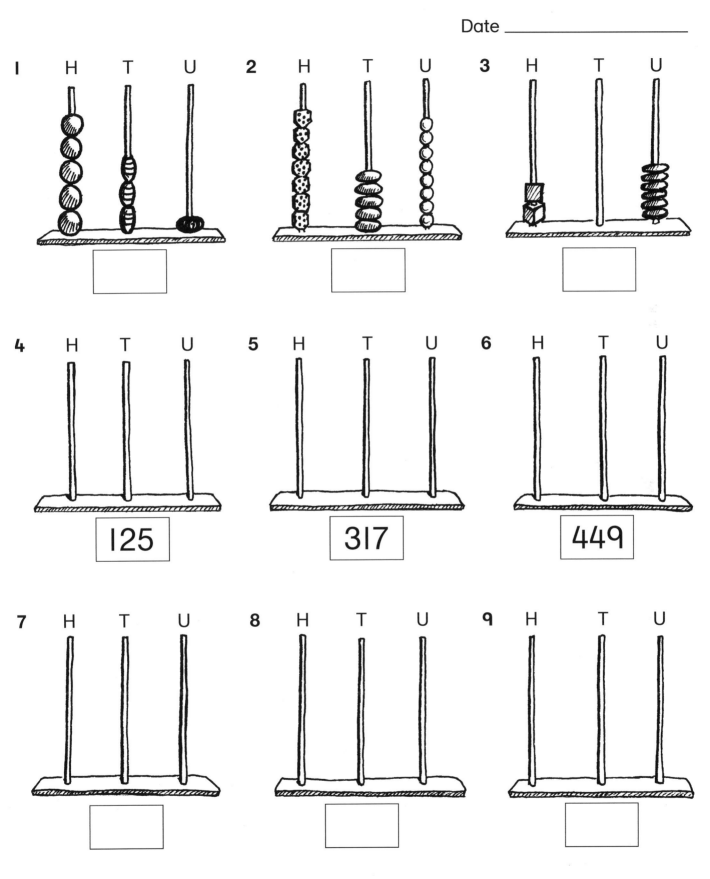

1   H   T   U

2   H   T   U

3   H   T   U

4   H   T   U

125

5   H   T   U

317

6   H   T   U

449

7   H   T   U

8   H   T   U

9   H   T   U

- (Compare and) order whole numbers to at least 1000, (say which is more or less, and give a number which lies between them).
- (Say the number that is 1, 10 or 100 more or less than any given number to at least 1000.)

Resources

Provide each child with the following:

- a copy of Activity 5 pupil sheet
- a pencil

Key words

zero, one, two…one thousand   more   less
small/smaller/smallest   large/larger/largest   between

Say to the children:

Listen carefully.

I am going to tell you some things to do.

I will say them only once, so listen very carefully.

Do only the things you are told to do and nothing else.

If you make a mistake, cross it out. Do not use an eraser.

There are 15 parts to this activity.

The activity

1. Look at the numbers 465 and 867. Which is more? Draw a ring around that number.

2. In the grey box, write a number that lies between 465 and 867.

3. Look at the numbers 132 and 312. Which is less? Draw a ring around that number.

4. In the grey box, write a number that lies between 132 and 312.

5. Look at the numbers 227 and 201. Which is smaller? Draw a ring around that number.

6. In the grey box, write a number that lies between 227 and 201.

7. Look at the numbers 509 and 519. Which is larger? Draw a ring around that number.

8. In the grey box, write a number that lies between 509 and 519.

9. Look at the numbers 445 and 355. Which is more? Draw a ring around that number.

10. In the grey box, write a number that lies between 445 and 355.

11. Look at the numbers 717 and 171. Which is less? Draw a ring around that number.

12. In the grey box, write a number that lies between 717 and 171.

13. Look at the numbers you have just drawn a ring around. In the boxes underneath, write these numbers in order, from smallest to largest.

14. Look at the function machine. This machine takes in numbers and then works out what is one, 10 and 100 more and less than that number. The machine has just broken down. Finish the machine's work by writing in the missing numbers.

15. Write your name at the top of the machine.

Answers

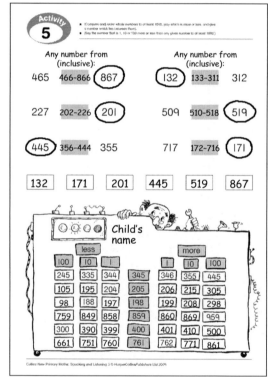

Discussion questions

↓ Look at the numbers 132 and 312. Which is less? (132)

↓ Tell me a number that lies between 227 and 201. (any number from 202 to 226 inclusive)

■ Look at the numbers you drew a ring around. Tell me these numbers in order, from smallest to largest. (132, 171, 201, 445, 519, 867)

■ Look at the function machine. Tell me the numbers that are one, 10, 100 more and less than 198. (199, 208, 298, 197, 188, 98)

↑ Think of the number 2418. What number is one more/10 more/100 more/one less/10 less/100 less? (2419/2428/2518/2417/2408/2318)

↑ Look at the numbers that went into the function machine. Tell me these numbers in order, from smallest to largest. (198, 205, 345, 400, 761, 859)

■ (Compare and) order whole numbers to at least 1000, (say which is more or less, and give a number which lies between them).
■ (Say the number that is 1, 10 or 100 more or less than any given number to at least 1000.)

Date _____

465		867	132		312
227		201	509		519
445		355	717		171

| | | | | | |

less | | | more
100	10	1		1	10	100
245	335	344	345	346	355	445
		204	205			
	188		198			
			859			959
300			400			
			761	762		

■ Round two-digit or three-digit numbers to the nearest 10 or 100.

Resources

Provide each child with the following:
- a copy of Activity 6 pupil sheet
- a pencil

Key words

zero, one, two…one hundred   one hundred, two hundred, three hundred… one thousand   round/rounded   nearest

Say to the children:

Listen carefully.

I am going to tell you some things to do.

I will say them only once, so listen very carefully.

Do only the things you are told to do and nothing else.

If you make a mistake, cross it out. Do not use an eraser.

There are 13 parts to this activity.

The activity

1. Round 47 to the nearest ten. Write the number 47 on the pot you rounded it to.

2. Round 63 to the nearest ten. Write the number 63 on the pot you rounded it to.

3. Round 138 to the nearest hundred. Write the number 138 on the pot you rounded it to.

4. Round 581 to the nearest hundred. Write the number 581 on the pot you rounded it to.

5. Round 85 to the nearest ten. Write the number 85 on the pot you rounded it to.

6. Round 352 to the nearest hundred. Write the number 352 on the pot you rounded it to.

7. Round 72 to the nearest ten. Write the number 72 on the pot you rounded it to.

8. Round 748 to the nearest hundred. Write the number 748 on the pot you rounded it to.

9. Round 24 to the nearest ten. Write the number 24 on the pot you rounded it to.

10. Round 56 to the nearest ten. Write the number 56 on the pot you rounded it to.

11. Round 260 to the nearest hundred. Write the number 260 on the pot you rounded it to.

12. Round 829 to the nearest hundred. Write the number 829 on the pot you rounded it to.

13. Round 33 to the nearest ten. Write your name on that pot.

Answers

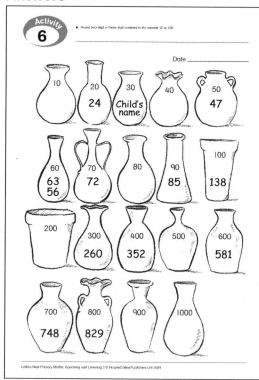

Discussion questions

↓ Choose a pot and tell me a number you wrote on it.

↓ When do you round a two-digit number up to the next multiple of 10? (When the units digit is 5, 6, 7, 8 or 9.)

■ Which number did you round to 90? (85)

■ Which multiple of ten did you round two numbers to? (60) What were these numbers? (56 and 63)

↑ Look at the pots that you did not write any numbers on. Choose a pot and tell me a number that you could write on it. (e.g. The 500 pot could have the number 503 written on it.)

↑ What is 348 rounded to the nearest hundred? (300) What is 348 rounded to the nearest ten? (350)

Round two-digit or three-digit numbers to the nearest 10 or 100.

Date _____

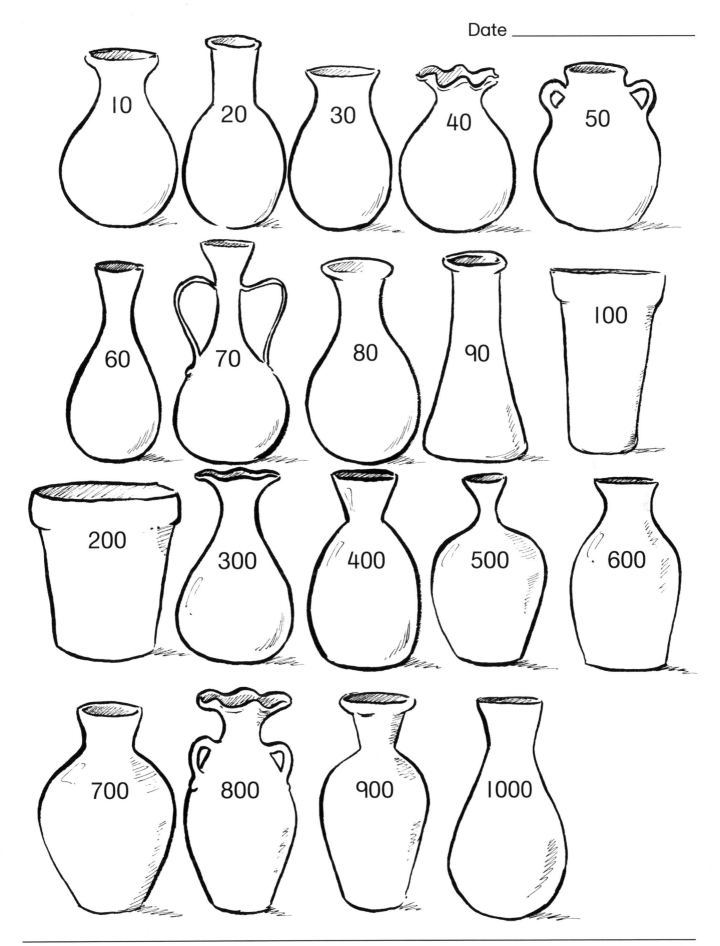

■ Read and write proper fractions, e.g. $\frac{3}{7}$, $\frac{9}{10}$, interpreting the denominator as the parts of a whole and the numerator as the number of parts.

Resources

Provide each child with the following:
■ a copy of Activity 7 pupil sheet   ■ a pencil
■ a coloured pencil

Key words

one, two, three…ten   fraction   divided   half/one half/halve
thirds, quarters, fifths, sixths, sevenths, eighths, ninths, tenths
first, second

Say to the children:

Listen carefully.

I am going to tell you some things to do.

I will say them only once, so listen very carefully.

Do only the things you are told to do and nothing else.

If you make a mistake, cross it out. Do not use an eraser.

There are 11 parts to this activity.

The activity

1. Look at the first Wheelo. Colour three quarters of the Wheelo.

2. Look at the second Wheelo. Colour five eighths of the Wheelo.

3. Look at the first Explosion. Colour seven tenths of the Explosion.

4. Look at the second Explosion. Colour two fifths of the Explosion.

5. Look at the first Mega. Colour two thirds of the Mega.

6. Look at the second Mega. Colour four sixths of the Mega.

7. Look at the first Diamond. What fraction of the Diamond is coloured? Write that fraction on the first Diamond.

8. Look at the first Diamond again. What fraction of the Diamond is not coloured? Write that fraction under the first Diamond.

9. Look at the second Diamond. What fraction of the Diamond is coloured? Write that fraction on the second Diamond.

10. Look at the second Diamond again. What fraction of the Diamond is not coloured? Write that fraction under the second Diamond.

11. Which chocolate bar has been divided into sixths? Write your name under that chocolate bar.

Answers

Discussion questions

↓ What fraction of the first Wheelo did you colour? ($\frac{3}{4}$ or $\frac{6}{8}$)

↓ What fraction of the first Mega did you not colour? ($\frac{1}{3}$ or $\frac{2}{6}$)

■ Look at the first Diamond. How many parts of this chocolate are coloured? (6) What fraction of the Diamond is coloured? ($\frac{3}{4}$ or $\frac{6}{8}$)

■ Which chocolate bars are divided into eighths? (Wheelo and Diamond) What fraction of these chocolates are coloured? (1st Wheelo — $\frac{3}{4}$ or $\frac{6}{8}$, 2nd Wheelo — $\frac{5}{8}$ and 1st Diamond — $\frac{3}{4}$ or $\frac{6}{8}$, 2nd Diamond — $\frac{3}{8}$)

↑ Look at the second Explosion. How much of this chocolate did you colour? ($\frac{2}{5}$) How else could you describe the amount of chocolate shaded? ($\frac{4}{10}$)

↑ Look at the second Mega. How much of this chocolate did you colour? ($\frac{4}{6}$) How else could you describe the amount of chocolate shaded? ($\frac{2}{3}$)

■ Read and write proper fractions, e.g. $\frac{3}{7}$, $\frac{9}{10}$, interpreting the denominator as the parts of a whole and the numerator as the number of parts.

Date _____

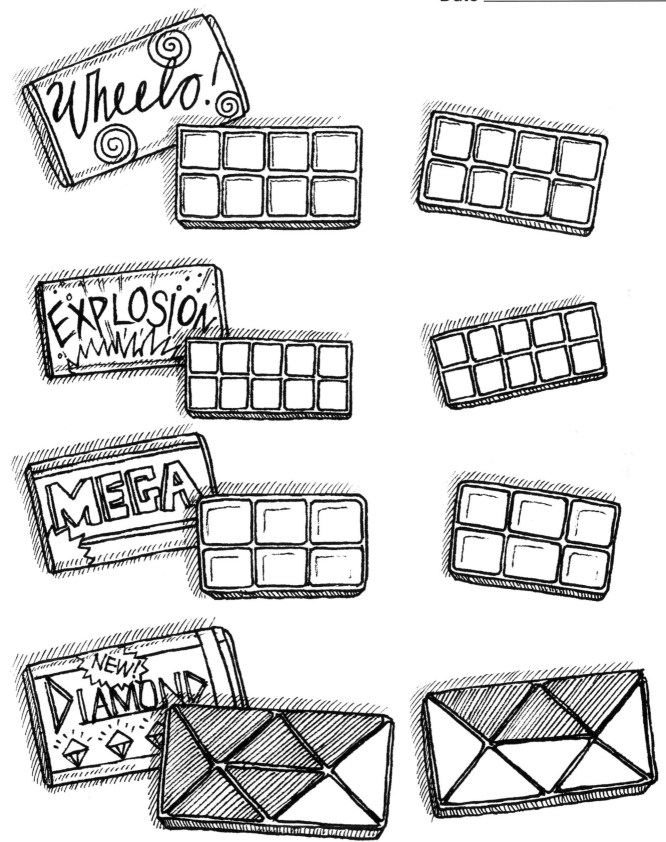

Year 3 Knowing and using number facts

■ Derive and recall all addition and subtraction facts for each number to 20.

Resources

Provide each child with the following:
- ■ a copy of Activity 8 pupil sheet
- ■ a pencil
- ■ a ruler (optional)

Key words

zero, one, two…twenty   add   plus   total   more   sum   double
subtract   minus   take away   difference   less   leaves   equals

Say to the children:

Listen carefully.

I am going to tell you some things to do.

I will say them only once, so listen very carefully.

Do only the things you are told to do and nothing else.

If you make a mistake, cross it out. Do not use an eraser.

There are 16 parts to this activity.

The activity

1. What is seven plus six? Find that number. What is eight add nine? Find that number. Now draw a line between these two numbers.

2. What is 15 subtract eight? Find that number. What is 14 minus five? Find that number. Now draw a line between these two numbers.

3. What is the difference between 18 and six? Find that number. What is 17 less nine? Find that number. Now draw a line between these two numbers.

4. What is double 10? Find that number. What is double five? Find that number. Now draw a line between these two numbers.

5. What is nine and six more? Find that number. What is 11 subtract eight? Find that number. Now draw a line between these two numbers.

6. What is eight add 11? Find that number. What is 14 minus 12? Find that number. Now draw a line between these two numbers.

7. What is eight plus six? Find that number. What is 20 subtract 10? Find that number. Now draw a line between these two numbers.

8. What is the difference between 17 and 12? Find that number. What is 14 less six? Find that number. Now draw a line between these two numbers.

9. What is nine subtract nine? Find that number. What is 15 take away 14? Find that number. Now draw a line between these two numbers.

10. What is four add nine? Find that number. What is 20 subtract 18? Find that number. Now draw a line between these two numbers.

11. What is five plus six? Find that number. What is eight less four? Find that number. Now draw a line between these two numbers.

12. What is 20 minus one? Find that number. What is the difference between 17 and three? Find that number. Now draw a line between these two numbers.

13. What is 13 subtract 13? Find that number. What is 10 and five more? Find that number. Now draw a line between these two numbers.

Answers

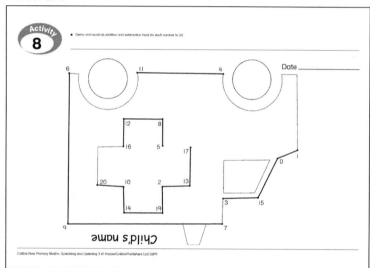

14. What is 20 minus 14? Find that number. What is 15 take away six? Find that number. Now draw a line between these two numbers.

15. What is double six? Find that number. What is 18 subtract two? Find that number. Now draw a line between these two numbers.

16. Turn your sheet upside down and write your name at the top of the picture.

Discussion questions

↓ What have you just drawn? (an ambulance) Is the drawing finished? (no)

↓ What is five add 13? (18) 14 minus eight? (6)

■ Who finished the drawing of the ambulance? Were you told to? (no)

■ When did you realise that you were drawing an ambulance?

↑ Did you make a mistake? Where? Do you know what your mistake was?

↑ What is five add nine? (14) If five add nine is 14, what is 15 add nine? (24) What about 25/35/75 add nine? (34/44/84)

■ Derive and recall all addition and subtraction facts for each number to 20.

Date _____

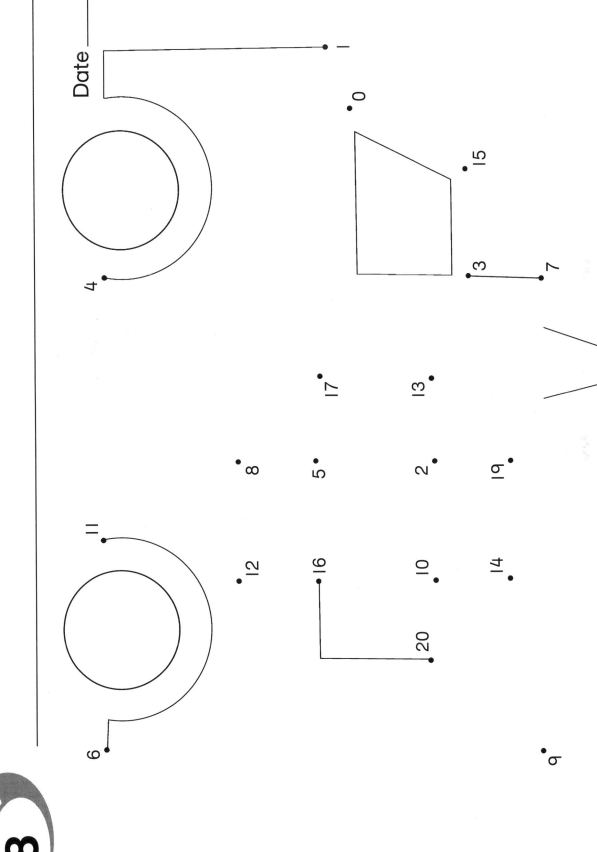

Activity 9

Year 3 Knowing and using number facts

■ Derive and recall multiplication facts for the 2, 3, 4, 5 and 10 times-tables and the corresponding division facts.

Resources

Provide each child with the following:
■ a copy of Activity 9 pupil sheet
■ a pencil

Key words

zero, one, two…one hundred   times   multiplied by   lots of   groups of   product of

Say to the children:

Listen carefully.

I am going to tell you some things to do.

I will say them only once, so listen very carefully.

Do only the things you are told to do and nothing else.

If you make a mistake, cross it out. Do not use an eraser.

There are 14 parts to this activity.

The activity

Look at the sheet. It shows a football pitch. This activity is like playing a game of football, but some of the rules are different. In our game there are 16 players a side and there are lots of goalkeepers. Circles are a team called Trenton Town and squares are Weston Wanderers. When a ball is passed from one player to another you draw a straight line. If the ball goes to a number in a circle in the shaded part of Trenton Town's net, it is a goal for Trenton Town. If the ball goes to a number in a square in the shaded part of Weston Wanderers' net, it is a goal for Weston Wanderers. Each goal scores one point.

1. Place your pencil on the dot at the word Start.

2. Pass the ball to the answer to ten times seven.

3. Ten times seven passes to three multiplied by three, and three multiplied by three passes to ten times ten.

4. Ten times ten passes to one multiplied by one, and one multiplied by one passes to two groups of five.

5. Two groups of five passes to the product of four and five, and the product of four and five passes to eight times four.

6. Eight times four passes to four lots of four, and four lots of four passes to four multiplied by three.

7. Four multiplied by three passes to two times two, and two times two passes to five groups of ten.

8. Five groups of ten passes to five times five, and five times five passes to the product of six and three.

9. The product of six and three passes to three lots of one, and three lots of one passes to nine multiplied by ten.

10. Nine multiplied by ten passes to three times seven, and three times seven passes to four times seven.

11. Four times seven passes to three groups of nine, and three groups of nine passes to five lots of one.

12. Five lots of one passes to six multiplied by four.

13. The whistle blows. Put each team's score in the box at the bottom of the sheet.

14. Write your name under the word Start.

Answers

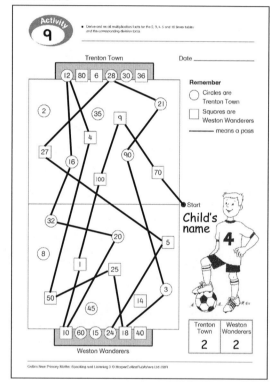

Discussion questions

↓ Who won the game? (It was a draw.)

↓ What is three times four/five multiplied by eight? (12/40)

■ Why didn't Weston Wanderers score three goals? (The last pass was 5 × 1 passes to 6 × 4, but 24 is in the opposing team.)

■ Choose a number from the Trenton Town team and tell me what two numbers multiplied together will give you that number.

↑ Choose a number from the sheet and tell me what number it is a multiple of. How do you know?

↑ Which numbers did not get to handle the ball during the game? (2, 6, 8, 14, 15, 30, 35, 36, 40, 45, 60, 80) Choose one of these numbers and put it into a multiplication calculation.

■ Derive and recall multiplication facts for the 2, 3, 4, 5 and 10 times-tables and the corresponding division facts.

Date _____

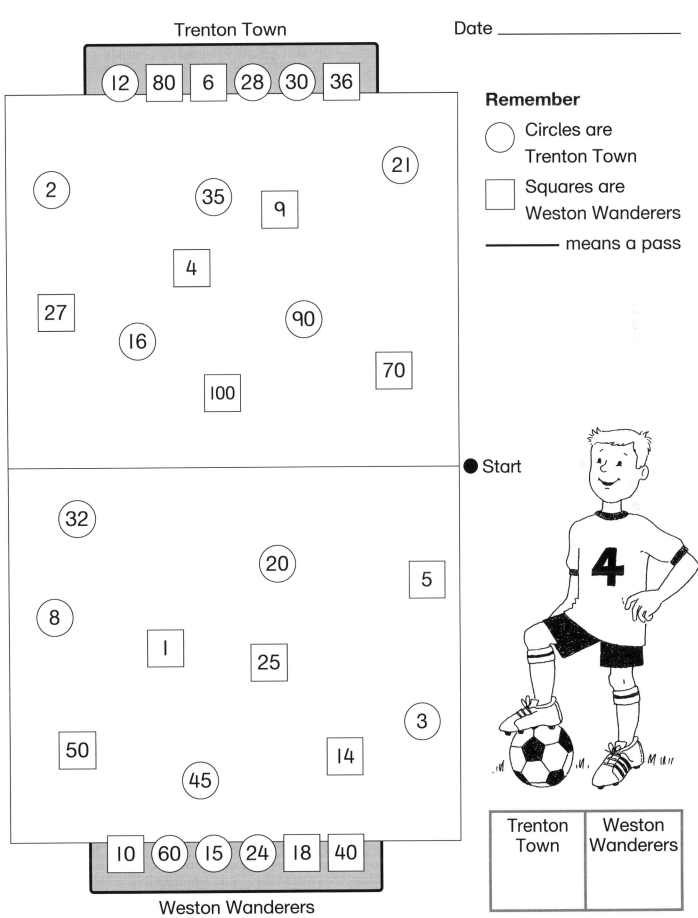

Trenton Town

⑫ 80 6 ㉘ ㉚ 36

Remember

◯ Circles are Trenton Town

▢ Squares are Weston Wanderers

——— means a pass

② ㉑ ㉟ 9

4

27 ⑯ ⑨⓪

70

100

● Start

㉜ ⑳ 5

⑧ 1 25

50 ③ 45 14

⑩ 60 ⑮ ㉔ 18 40

Weston Wanderers

Trenton Town	Weston Wanderers

■ Derive and recall division facts corresponding to the 2, 5 and 10 times-tables.

Resources

Provide each child with the following:
- a copy of Activity 10 pupil sheet
- a red, blue, green, yellow and orange coloured pencil

Key words

zero, one, two, one hundred   calculations   division   divided by

Say to the children:

Listen carefully.

I am going to tell you some things to do.

I will say them only once, so listen very carefully.

Do only the things you are told to do and nothing else.

If you make a mistake, cross it out. Do not use an eraser.

There are 11 parts to this activity.

The activity

1. Three of the calculations on the sheet have an answer of one. Find these calculations and colour the shapes red.

2. Three of the calculations have an answer of ten. Find these calculations and colour the shapes red.

3. Three of the calculations have an answer of four. Find these calculations and colour the shapes blue.

4. Three of the calculations have an answer of eight. Find these calculations and colour the shapes blue.

5. Three of the calculations have an answer of two. Find these calculations and colour the shapes green.

6. Three of the calculations have an answer of six. Find these calculations and colour the shapes green.

7. Three of the calculations have an answer of five. Find these calculations and colour the shapes yellow.

8. Three of the calculations have an answer of nine. Find these calculations and colour the shapes yellow.

9. Three of the calculations have an answer of three. Find these calculations and colour the shapes orange.

10. Three of the calculations have an answer of seven. Find these calculations and colour the shapes orange.

11. Write your name at the top of the sheet.

Answers

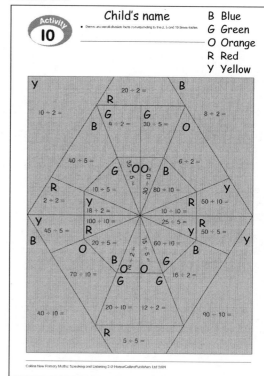

Discussion questions

↓ How many parts of the pattern are coloured blue? (6)

↓ What is 40 divided by five/10? (8/4)

■ What colour are the calculations with an answer of six? (green)

■ Which shapes did you colour yellow? (those with an answer of 5 and 9)

↑ As we got towards the end of the activity, could you tell which shapes were going to be coloured yellow and orange? Why?

↑ 16 divided by two is eight. What other division and multiplication facts do you know using these three numbers? ($16 \div 8 = 2$; $2 \times 8 = 16$; $8 \times 2 = 16$)

■ Derive and recall division facts corresponding to the 2, 5 and 10 times-tables.

Date _____

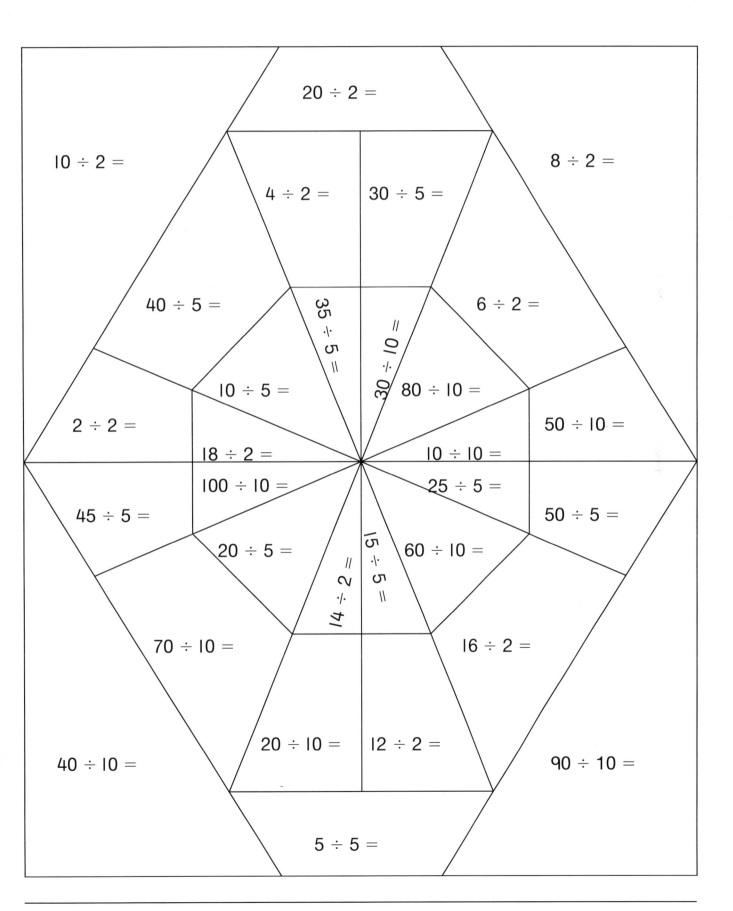

$20 \div 2 =$

$10 \div 2 =$

$8 \div 2 =$

$4 \div 2 =$

$30 \div 5 =$

$40 \div 5 =$

$35 \div 5 =$

$30 \div 10 =$

$6 \div 2 =$

$10 \div 5 =$

$80 \div 10 =$

$2 \div 2 =$

$50 \div 10 =$

$18 \div 2 =$

$10 \div 10 =$

$100 \div 10 =$

$25 \div 5 =$

$45 \div 5 =$

$50 \div 5 =$

$20 \div 5 =$

$15 \div 5 =$

$60 \div 10 =$

$14 \div 2 =$

$70 \div 10 =$

$16 \div 2 =$

$20 \div 10 =$

$12 \div 2 =$

$40 \div 10 =$

$90 \div 10 =$

$5 \div 5 =$

■ Recognise multiples of 2, 5 or 10 up to 1000 (and three-digit multiples of 50 and 100).

Resources

Provide each child with the following:
- a copy of Activity 11 pupil sheet
- a pencil
- a coloured pencil

Key words

zero, one, two…one thousand   multiples
first, second, third, fourth, fifth

Say to the children:

Listen carefully.

I am going to tell you some things to do.

I will say them only once, so listen very carefully.

Do only the things you are told to do and nothing else.

If you make a mistake, cross it out. Do not use an eraser.

There are 11 parts to this activity.

The activity

1. Look at the surfboards on the first line of waves. Colour all the numbers that are multiples of five.

2. Look at the empty surfboard at the end of the first line. Write a number on the surfboard that is another multiple of five.

3. Look at the surfboards on the second line of waves. Colour all the numbers that are multiples of 10.

4. Look at the empty surfboard at the end of the second line. Write a number on the surfboard that is another multiple of 10.

5. Look at the surfboards on the third line of waves. Colour all the numbers that are multiples of two.

6. Look at the empty surfboard at the end of the third line. Write a number on the surfboard that is another multiple of two.

7. Look at the surfboards on the fourth line of waves. Colour all the numbers that are multiples of 50.

8. Look at the empty surfboard at the end of the fourth line. Write a number on the surfboard that is another multiple of 50.

9. Look at the surfboards on the fifth line of waves. Colour all the numbers that are multiples of 100.

10. Look at the empty surfboard at the end of the fifth line. Write a number on the surfboard that is another multiple of 100.

11. Look back at the first line of waves. Write your name above a number that is a multiple of two.

Answers

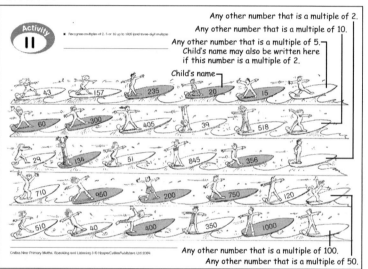

Any other number that is a multiple of 2.
Any other number that is a multiple of 10.
Any other number that is a multiple of 5. Child's name may also be written here if this number is a multiple of 2.
Child's name
Any other number that is a multiple of 100.
Any other number that is a multiple of 50.

Discussion questions

↓ Which numbers did you colour on the third wave? (134 and 356)

↓ Look at the last wave. Which numbers are multiples of 100? (400 and 1000)

■ How many numbers did you colour on the fourth wave? (3) What were the numbers? (950, 200 and 750) What do you know about these three numbers? (multiples of 50)

■ Which other numbers did you write down as multiples of five/10/ two/50/100?

↑ Look at all the numbers on the sheet. How many numbers are multiples of 10? (16) Which numbers are multiples of 10? (20, 60, 300, 710, 950, 200, 750, 120, 510, 40, 400, 350, 1000 and the three numbers written by the child as multiples of 10, 50 and 100)

↑ How do you know if a number is a multiple of five/10/two/50/100? (5 – end in 0 or 5; 10 – end in 0; 2 – end in 0, 2, 4, 6, 8; 50 – end in 00 or 50; 100 – end in 00)

- Recognise multiples of 2, 5 or 10 up to 1000 (and three-digit multiples of 50 and 100).

Date _____

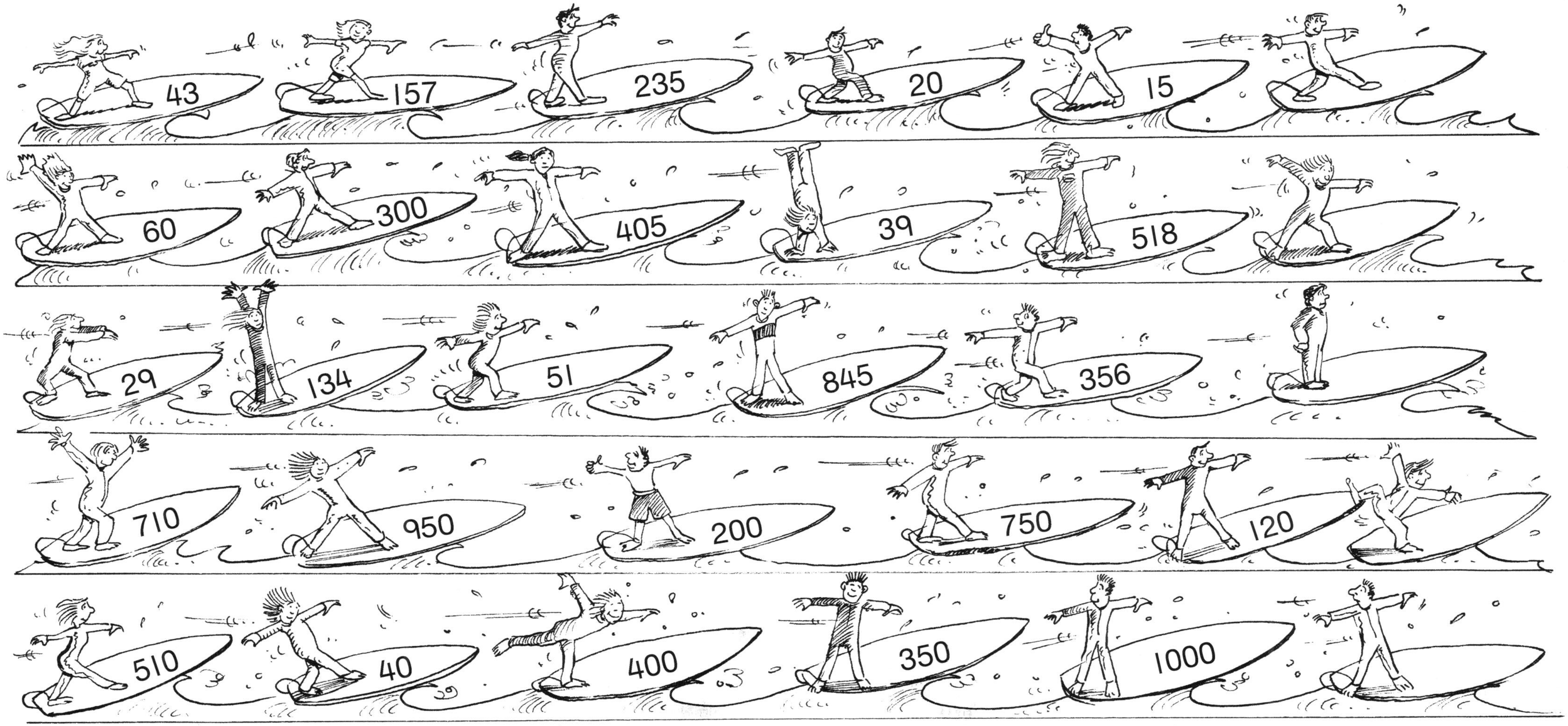

43 157 235 20 15

60 300 405 39 518

29 134 51 845 356

710 950 200 750 120

510 40 400 350 1000

- Use knowledge of number operations and corresponding inverses, including doubling and halving.
- (Derive and recall doubles of whole numbers to at least 20, multiples of 5 to 100, multiples of 50 to 500, and the corresponding halves.)

Resources

Provide each child with the following:
- a copy of Activity 12 pupil sheet
- a red, blue, green, yellow and orange coloured pencil

Key words

zero, one, two…one thousand   double   twice   times   multiplied by   lots of   groups of   product   half/halve   divided by   between

Say to the children:

Listen carefully.

I am going to tell you some things to do.

I will say them only once, so listen very carefully.

Do only the things you are told to do and nothing else.

If you make a mistake, cross it out. Do not use an eraser.

There are 21 parts to this activity.

The activity

1. What is double seven? Colour that number red in Doubles Tower.

2. What is half of 32? Colour that number red in Halves Court.

3. What is twice 80? Colour that number red in Doubles Tower.

4. What is 140 divided by two? Colour that number red in Halves Court.

5. What is 250 multiplied by two? Colour that number blue in Doubles Tower.

6. What is half of 300? Colour that number blue in Halves Court.

7. What is two lots of 13? Colour that number blue in Doubles Tower.

8. What is 12 divided by two? Colour that number blue in Halves Court.

9. What is two groups of 45? Colour that number green in Doubles Tower.

10. What is half of 70? Colour that number green in Halves Court.

11. What is the product of 100 and two? Colour that number green in Doubles Tower.

12. What is 900 divided by two? Colour that number green in Halves Court.

13. What is double 350? Colour that number yellow in Doubles Tower.

14. What is half of 28? Colour that number yellow in Halves Court.

15. What is twice 11? Colour that number yellow in Doubles Tower.

16. What it 600 divided by two? Colour that number yellow in Halves Court.

17. What is 25 multiplied by two? Colour that number orange in Doubles Tower.

18. What is half of 190? Colour that number orange in Halves Court.

19. What is double nine? Colour that number orange in Doubles Tower.

20. What is eight divided by two? Colour that number orange in Halves Court.

21. Write your name between Doubles Tower and Halves Court.

Answers

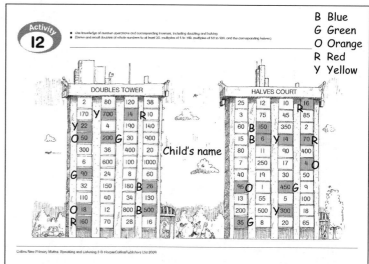

Discussion questions

↓ Which numbers did you colour red in the Doubles Tower? (14 and 160)

↓ What colour is the number six in Halves Court? (blue)

■ What is half of 170? (85) Did you colour this number in Halves Court? (no)

■ Tell me the numbers you coloured in Doubles Tower/Halves Court. (14, 18, 22, 26, 50, 90, 160, 200, 500, 700/4, 6, 14, 16, 35, 70, 95, 150, 300, 450)

↑ Choose a number in Doubles Tower/ Halves Court you have not coloured and double/halve that number.

↑ Choose a number you have coloured. Can you keep doubling/halving that number?

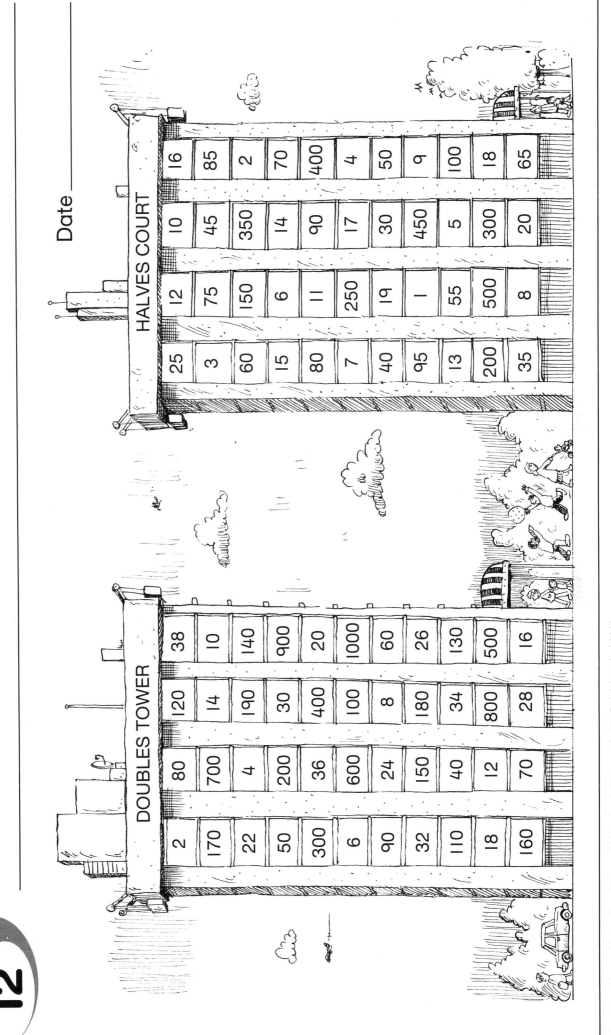

Use knowledge of number operations and corresponding inverses, including doubling and halving.

(Derive and recall doubles of whole numbers to at least 20, multiples of 50 to 500, multiples of 5 to 100, and the corresponding halves.)

Date

HALVES COURT

16	10	12	25
85	45	75	3
2	350	150	60
70	14	6	15
400	90	11	80
4	17	250	7
50	30	19	40
9	450	1	95
100	5	55	13
18	300	500	200
65	20	8	35

DOUBLES TOWER

38	120	80	2
10	14	700	170
140	190	4	22
900	30	200	50
20	400	36	300
1000	100	600	6
60	8	24	90
26	180	150	32
130	34	40	110
500	800	12	18
16	28	70	160

Year 3 Calculating

- Add mentally combinations of one-digit, two-digit (and three-digit numbers and multiples of 10 and 100).

Resources

Provide each child with the following:
- a copy of Activity 13 pupil sheet
- a pencil
- a ruler (optional)

Key words

zero, one, two… one thousand   add   plus   total   more   sum   double   equals

Say to the children:

Listen carefully.

I am going to tell you some things to do.

I will say them only once, so listen very carefully.

Do only the things you are told to do and nothing else.

If you make a mistake, cross it out. Do not use an eraser.

There are 17 parts to this activity.

The activity

1. What is 40 plus 70? Find that number. What is 300 add 16? Find that number. Now draw a line between these two numbers.

2. What is 365 and four more? Find that number. What is 60 add 32? Find that number. Now draw a line between these two numbers.

3. What is the total of 43 and 25? Find that number. What is 78 and 10 more? Find that number. Now draw a line between these two numbers.

4. What is 10 more than 274? Find that number. What is 52 add 80? Find that number. Now draw a line between these two numbers.

5. What is the sum of 400 and 800? Find that number. What is one more than 629? Find that number. Now draw a line between these two numbers.

6. What is 400 plus 37? Find that number. What is 60 add 66? Find that number. Now draw a line between these two numbers.

7. What is the sum of 33 and 24? Find that number. What is the total of 93 and 10? Find that number. Now draw a line between these two numbers.

8. What is double 60? Find that number. What is 40 add 52? Find that number. Now draw a line between these two numbers.

9. What is 700 plus 800? Find that number. What is 216 add 100? Find that number. Now draw a line between these two numbers.

10. What is six more than 543? Find that number. What is 42 plus 15? Find that number. Now draw a line between these two numbers.

11. What is the sum of 83 and 20? Find that number. What is 100 more than 184? Find that number. Now draw a line between these two numbers.

12. What is double 600? Find that number. What is 32 add 36? Find that number. Now draw a line between these two numbers.

13. What is 90 plus 30? Find that number. What is 10 more than 116? Find that number. Now draw a line between these two numbers.

14. What is 530 add 100? Find that number. What is 69 plus 300? Find that number. Now draw a line between these two numbers.

15. What is the total of 92 and 40? Find that number. What is the sum of 432 and five? Find that number. Now draw a line between these two numbers.

16. What is 50 add 60? Find that number. What is 540 plus nine? Find that number. Now draw a line between these two numbers.

17. Write your name inside the object you have just drawn.

Answers

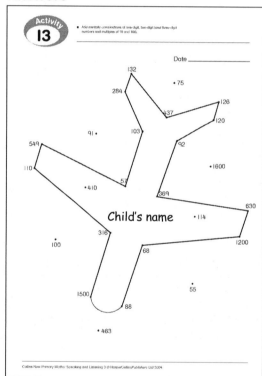

Discussion questions

⬇ What have you just drawn? (an aeroplane)

⬇ What is 40 add 70? (110) What is another way of saying this calculation? (e.g. 40 plus 70, 40 and 70 more…)

■ When did you realise that you were drawing an aeroplane?

■ Did you make a mistake? Where? Do you know what your mistake was?

↑ What calculations did you find easy/hard?

↑ Choose one of the numbers you did not use to draw the aeroplane and put it in an addition calculation.

■ Add mentally combinations of one-digit, two-digit (and three-digit numbers and multiples of 10 and 100).

Date _____

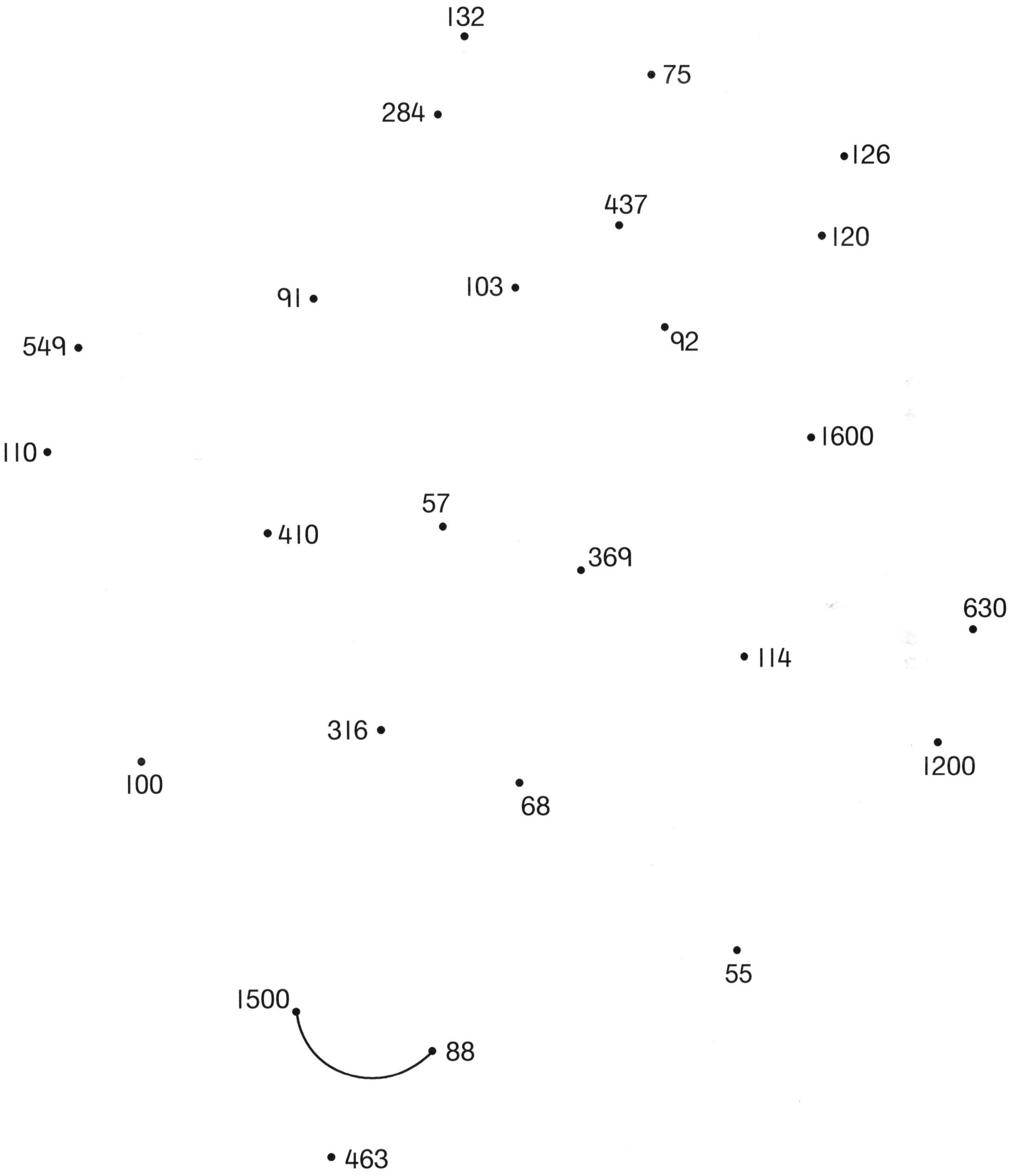

132

• 75

284 •

•126

437

•120

91 •   103 •

549 •   •92

110 •

•1600

57

• 410   •

                .369

                                    630

                        • 114

316 •

                                    •
                                    1200

100

        68

                        •
                        55

1500

        88

• 463

■ Subtract mentally combinations of one-digit, two-digit (and three-digit numbers and multiples of 10 and 100).

Resources

Provide each child with the following:
■ a copy of Activity 14 pupil sheet
■ a pencil

Key words

zero, one, two…one thousand subtract minus take away difference less leaves equals multiple

Say to the children:

Listen carefully.

I am going to tell you some things to do.

I will say them only once, so listen very carefully.

Do only the things you are told to do and nothing else.

If you make a mistake, cross it out. Do not use an eraser.

There are 13 parts to this activity.

The activity

1. Look at canoe A. What is 456 take away 10? Draw a ring around that number.

2. Look at canoe A again. What is 459 subtract four? Draw a cross through that number.

3. Look at canoe B. What is 1200 minus 300? Draw a ring around that number.

4. Look at canoe B again. What is the difference between 1500 and 800? Draw a cross through that number.

5. Look at canoe C. What is 120 less 40? Draw a ring around that number.

6. Look at canoe C again. What is 160 take away 90? Draw a cross through that number.

7. Look at canoe D. What is 112 minus 50? Draw a ring around that number.

8. Look at canoe D again. What is the difference between 87 and 26? Draw a cross through that number.

9. Look at canoe E. What is 604 less 100? Draw a ring around that number.

10. Look at canoe E again. What is 513 subtract seven? Draw a cross through that number.

11. Look at canoe F. What is 700 minus four? Draw a ring around that number.

12. Look at canoe F again. What is the difference between 786 and 100? Draw a cross through that number.

13. Look at all the numbers you drew a ring around. Write your name under the number that is a multiple of 100.

Answers

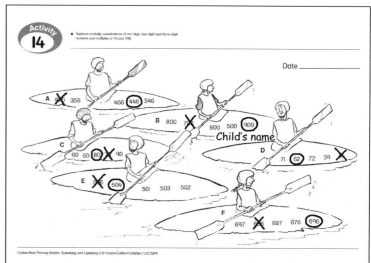

Discussion questions

↓ Which number did you draw a cross through on the first canoe? (455)

↓ What is the smallest/largest number you drew a ring around? (62/900)

■ Which number did you write your name under? (900). What is 900 a multiple of? (100) Is it a multiple of anything else? (e.g. 50, 10, 5, 2)

■ What is the difference between 87 and 26? (61) What did you do to that number? (drew a cross through it)

↑ What calculations did you find easy/hard? Why?

↑ Choose one of the numbers you did not draw a ring around or a cross through and put it in a subtraction calculation.

■ Subtract mentally combinations of one-digit, two-digit (and three-digit numbers and multiples of 10 and 100).

Date _____

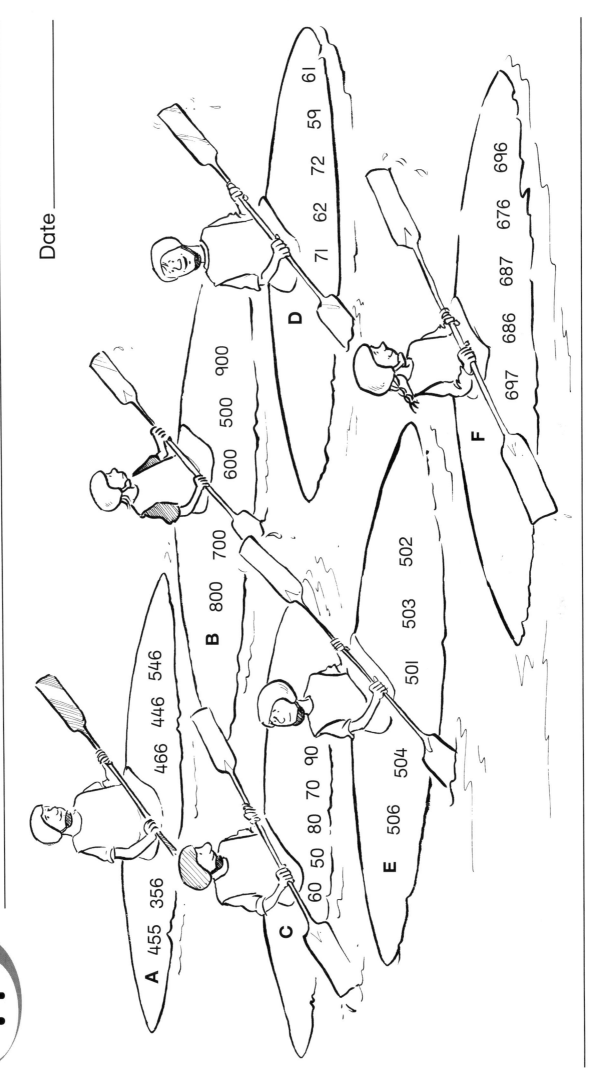

A 455 356

466 446 546

B 800 700

600 500 900

C 60 50 80 70 90

D 71 62 72 59 61

E 506 504 501 503 502

F 697 686 687 676 696

■ Add or subtract mentally combinations of one-digit, two-digit (and three-digit numbers and multiples of 10 and 100).

Resources

Provide each child with the following:

■ a copy of Activity 15 pupil sheet

■ a pencil

Key words

zero, one, two…one thousand add plus total more sum double subtract minus take away difference less leaves equals

Say to the children:

Listen carefully.

I am going to tell you some things to do.

I will say them only once, so listen very carefully.

Do only the things you are told to do and nothing else.

If you make a mistake, cross it out. Do not use an eraser.

There are 16 parts to this activity.

The activity

1. Write your name at the top of the sheet.

2. Find calculation one. Work out the missing number and write it in the circle.

3. Now find the same number in one of the grey boxes at the sides. In this box there is a letter. Write this letter in box one at the bottom of the sheet.

4. Find calculation twelve. Work out the missing number and write it in the circle. Now find the letter with that answer and write it in box nine.

5. Find calculation eight. Work out the missing number and write it in the circle. Now find the letter with that answer and write it in box sixteen.

6. Find calculation four. Work out the missing number and write it in the circle. Now find the letter with that answer and write it in box twelve.

7. Find calculation six. Work out the missing number and write it in the circle. Now find the letter with that answer and write it in boxes four and thirty.

8. Find calculation ten. Work out the missing number and write it in the circle. Now find the letter with that answer and write it in boxes six and twenty-four.

9. Find calculation seven. Work out the missing number and write it in the circle. Now find the letter with that answer and write it in box twenty.

10. Find calculation two. Work out the missing number and write it in the circle. Now find the letter with that answer and write it in boxes seven, eleven and twenty-eight.

11. Find calculation five. Work out the missing number and write it in the circle. Now find the letter with that answer and write it in box twenty-six.

12. Find calculation thirteen. Work out the missing number and write it in the circle. Now find the letter with that answer and write it in boxes two, eight, seventeen, twenty-two and twenty-seven.

13. Find calculation nine. Work out the missing number and write it in the circle. Now find the letter with that answer and write it in box thirty-two.

14. Find calculation three. Work out the missing number and write it in the circle. Now find the letter with that answer and write it in box twenty-one.

15. Find calculation eleven. Work out the missing number and write it in the circle. Now find the letter with that answer and write it in boxes five, fifteen, eighteen, twenty-three, twenty-nine and thirty-one.

16. Find calculation fourteen. Work out the missing number and write it in the circle. Now find the letter with that answer and write it in box fourteen.

Answers

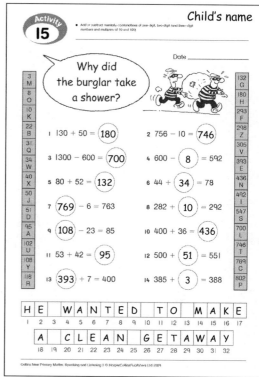

Discussion questions

↓ Why did the burglar take a shower? (He wanted to make a clean getaway.)

↓ Tell me the answer to one of the calculations you did.

■ Choose a calculation you did and explain how you worked it out. Did anyone work out this calculation in a different way?

■ Look at calculation nine. What is the missing number? (108) How did you work it out? Did anyone work it out using a different method?

↑ Look at all the calculations on the sheet. Which calculations do you find easy/hard?

↑ Look at calculation eleven. What is the answer? (95) What is 95 subtract 42? (53) How do you know?

■ Add or subtract mentally combinations of one-digit, two-digit (and three-digit numbers and multiples of 10 and 100).

Date _____

Why did the burglar take a shower?

3 M	132 G
8 O	180 H
10 K	293 F
22 B	298 Z
31 Q	305 V
34 W	393 E
40 X	436 N
50 J	492 I
51 D	547 S
95 A	700 L
102 U	746 T
108 Y	769 C
118 R	802 P

1 $130 + 50 = \bigcirc$

2 $756 - 10 = \bigcirc$

3 $1300 - 600 = \bigcirc$

4 $600 - \bigcirc = 592$

5 $80 + 52 = \bigcirc$

6 $44 + \bigcirc = 78$

7 $\bigcirc - 6 = 763$

8 $282 + \bigcirc = 292$

9 $\bigcirc - 23 = 85$

10 $400 + 36 = \bigcirc$

11 $53 + 42 = \bigcirc$

12 $500 + \bigcirc = 551$

13 $\bigcirc + 7 = 400$

14 $385 + \bigcirc = 388$

1	2	3	4	5	6	7	8	9	10	11	12	13	14	15	16	17

18	19	20	21	22	23	24	25	26	27	28	29	30	31	32

Year 3 Calculating

- Add or subtract mentally combinations of one-digit, two-digit (and three-digit numbers and multiples of 10 and 100).

Resources

Provide each child with the following:
- a copy of Activity 16 pupil sheet
- a pencil

Key words

zero, one, two…one thousand   add   plus   total   more   sum   double   subtract   minus   take away   difference   less   leaves   equals   smallest   largest

Say to the children:

Listen carefully.

I am going to tell you some things to do.

I will say them only once, so listen very carefully.

Do only the things you are told to do and nothing else.

If you make a mistake, cross it out. Do not use an eraser.

There are 14 parts to this activity.

The activity

1. Look at the numbers in row a. Add the largest number to the smallest number. Write the answer on ball one.

2. Look at the numbers in row a again. Subtract the smallest number from the largest number. Write the answer on ball two.

3. Look at the numbers in row b. Add the largest number to the smallest number. Write the answer on ball three.

4. Look at the numbers in row b again. Find the difference between the first two numbers. Write the answer on ball four.

5. Look at the numbers in row c. Find the difference between the first two numbers. Write the answer on ball five.

6. Write your name on ball six.

7. Look at the numbers in row d. What is the total of the first two numbers? Write the answer on ball seven.

8. Look at the numbers in row d again. Subtract the smallest number from the largest number. Write the answer on ball eight.

9. Look at the numbers in row e. Add the largest number to the smallest number. Write the answer on ball nine.

10. Look at the numbers in row e again. Subtract the smallest number from the largest number. Write the answer on ball ten.

11. Look at the numbers in row f. Add the first two numbers together. Write the answer on ball eleven.

12. Look at the numbers in row f again. Subtract the smallest number from the largest number. Write the answer on ball twelve.

13. Look at the numbers in row g. What is the total of the first two numbers? Write the answer on ball thirteen.

14. Look at the numbers in row g again. Find the difference between the first two numbers. Write the answer on ball fourteen.

Answers

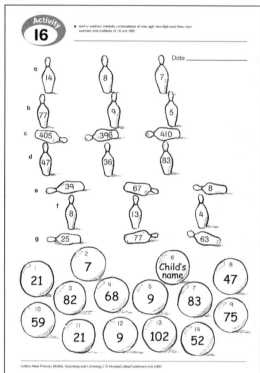

Discussion questions

↓ What number have you written on ball seven? (83)

↓ On which ball did you write the number 59? (10)

■ What do you notice about the numbers you have written on balls one and eleven? (both 21)

■ Look at all the numbers in row e. Choose any two numbers and add them together. Choose another two numbers and find the difference between them.

↑ Look at the numbers in row d. What are they? (47, 36, 83) What can you tell me about these three numbers? ($47 + 36 = 83$, $36 + 47 = 83$, $83 - 47 = 36$ and $83 - 36 = 47$)

↑ Look at the numbers on the balls. Choose any two numbers and add them together. What is the difference between these two numbers?

■ Add or subtract mentally combinations of one-digit, two-digit (and three-digit numbers and multiples of 10 and 100).

Date _____

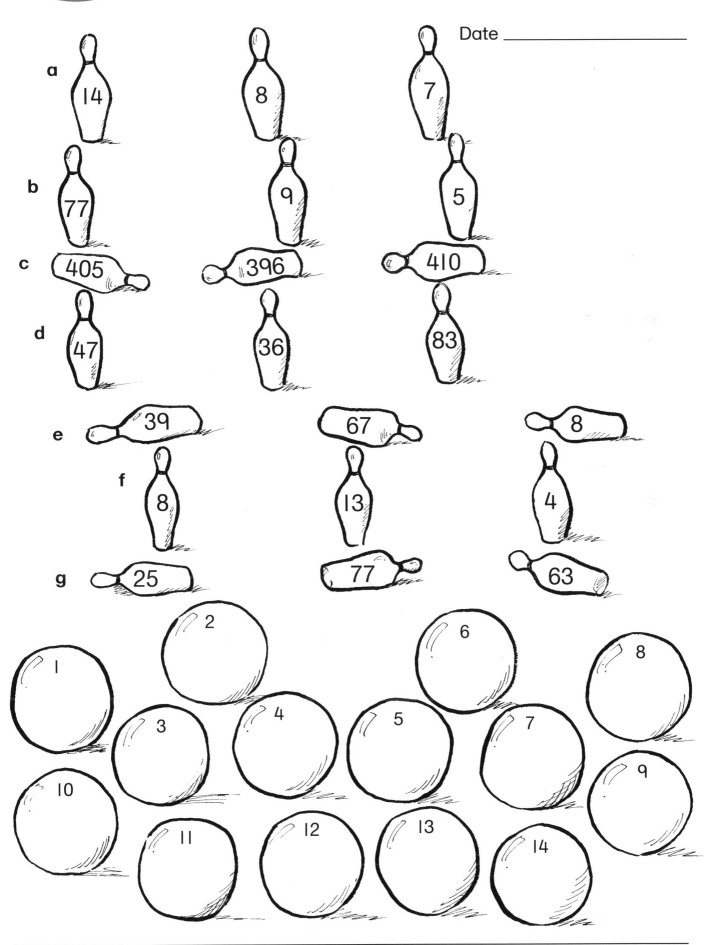

a   14   8   7

b   77   9   5

c   405   396   410

d   47   36   83

e   39   67   8

f   8   13   4

g   25   77   63

1   2   3   4   5   6   7   8   9   10   11   12   13   14

- Develop and use written methods to record, support or explain addition of two-digit and three-digit numbers

Resources

Provide each child with the following:
- a copy of Activity 17 pupil sheet
- a pencil

Key words

zero, one, two…one thousand   tens   smallest   largest   add   addition   plus   equals

Say to the children:

Listen carefully.

I am going to tell you some things to do.

I will say them only once, so listen very carefully.

Do only the things you are told to do and nothing else.

If you make a mistake, cross it out. Do not use an eraser.

There are 8 parts to this activity.

The activity

1. Look at the calculations in row A. Draw a ring around the calculation you think will have the smallest answer.

2. Now answer all the calculations in row A.

3. Look at the calculations in row B. Draw a cross above the calculation you think will have the largest answer.

4. Now answer all the calculations in row B.

5. Look at the calculations in row C. Draw a ring around the calculation you think will have the smallest answer and a cross above the calculation you think will have the largest answer.

6. Now answer all the calculations in row C.

7. In row D, write an addition calculation where the answer is 349.

8. Look at the answers to all of the calculations. Write your name under the answer that has a nine in the tens place.

Answers

Discussion questions

↓ Which calculation did you draw a ring around in row A? Was it the smallest answer?

↓ Choose a calculation and tell me the answer.

■ Which answer has a nine in the tens place? (892)
What did you do under that answer? (wrote their name)

■ What are the answers to the calculations in row C? (811, 741, 892, 720)

↑ What calculation did you write in row D? Who wrote a different one?

↑ Did you get any calculations wrong? Which ones? Do you know why you got the wrong answer? What will you do next time you see a calculation similar to this?

■ Develop and use written methods to record, support or explain addition of two-digit and three-digit numbers.

Date _____

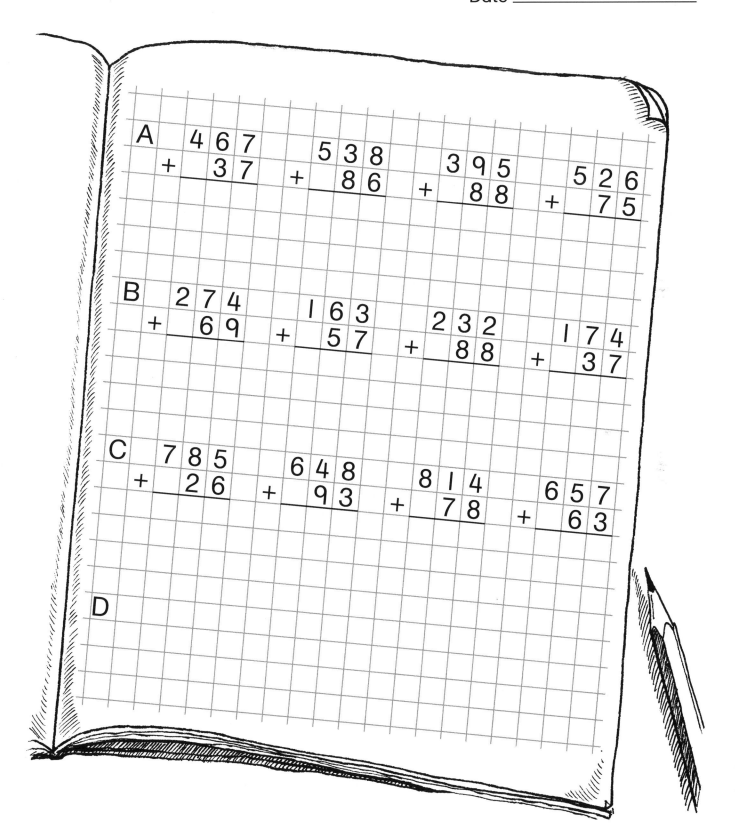

A
$$
\begin{array}{r}
467 \\
+37 \\
\hline
\end{array}
\qquad
\begin{array}{r}
538 \\
+86 \\
\hline
\end{array}
\qquad
\begin{array}{r}
395 \\
+88 \\
\hline
\end{array}
\qquad
\begin{array}{r}
526 \\
+75 \\
\hline
\end{array}
$$

B
$$
\begin{array}{r}
274 \\
+69 \\
\hline
\end{array}
\qquad
\begin{array}{r}
163 \\
+57 \\
\hline
\end{array}
\qquad
\begin{array}{r}
232 \\
+88 \\
\hline
\end{array}
\qquad
\begin{array}{r}
174 \\
+37 \\
\hline
\end{array}
$$

C
$$
\begin{array}{r}
785 \\
+26 \\
\hline
\end{array}
\qquad
\begin{array}{r}
648 \\
+93 \\
\hline
\end{array}
\qquad
\begin{array}{r}
814 \\
+78 \\
\hline
\end{array}
\qquad
\begin{array}{r}
657 \\
+63 \\
\hline
\end{array}
$$

D

Year 3 Calculating

■ Develop and use written methods to record, support or explain subtraction of two-digit and three-digit numbers.

Resources

Provide each child with the following:
■ a copy of Activity 18 pupil sheet
■ a pencil

Key words

zero, one, two…one thousand   smallest   largest   subtract
minus   take away   difference   less   between   leaves   equals

Say to the children:

Listen carefully.

I am going to tell you some things to do.

I will say them only once, so listen very carefully.

Do only the things you are told to do and nothing else.

If you make a mistake, cross it out. Do not use an eraser.

There are 8 parts to this activity.

The activity

1. Look at the calculations in row A. Draw a ring around the calculation you think will have the largest answer.

2. Now answer all the calculations in row A.

3. Look at the calculations in row B. Draw a cross above the calculation you think will have the smallest answer.

4. Now answer all the calculations in row B.

5. Look at the calculations in row C. Draw a ring around the calculation you think will have the largest answer and a cross above the calculation you think will have the smallest answer.

6. Now answer all the calculations in row C.

7. In row D, write a subtraction calculation where the answer is 537.

8. Look at the answers to all of the calculations. Write your name under the answer that is between 300 and 400.

Answers

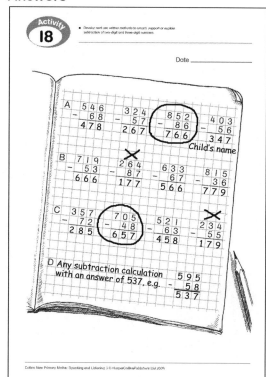

Discussion questions

↓ Which calculations did you draw a ring around in row A? Was it the largest answer?

↓ Choose a calculation and tell me the answer.

■ Which answer is between 300 and 400? (347) What did you do to that answer? (Wrote their name underneath it.)

■ What are the answers to the calculations in row B? (666, 177, 566, 779) What do you notice about all the answers in row B? (In each answer at least two of the digits are the same.)

↑ What calculation did you write in row D? Who wrote a different one?

↑ Did you get any calculations wrong? Which ones? Do you know why you got the wrong answer? What will you do next time you see a calculation similar to this?

■ Develop and use written methods to record, support or explain subtraction of two-digit and three-digit numbers.

Date _____

```
A     5 4 6        3 2 4        8 5 2        4 0 3
    -   6 8      -   5 7      -   8 6      -   5 6


B     7 1 9        2 6 4        6 3 3        8 1 5
    -   5 3      -   8 7      -   6 7      -   3 6


C     3 5 7        7 0 5        5 2 1        2 3 4
    -   7 2      -   4 8      -   6 3      -   5 5


D
```

■ Develop and use written methods to record, support or explain addition and subtraction of two-digit and three-digit numbers.

Resources

Provide each child with the following:
■ a copy of Activity 19 pupil sheet
■ a pencil

Key words

zero, one, two…one thousand   calculation   add, addition   plus
subtract, subtraction   minus   take away   answer   sign
largest   smallest

Say to the children:

Listen carefully.

I am going to tell you some things to do.

I will say them only once, so listen very carefully.

Do only the things you are told to do and nothing else.

If you make a mistake, cross it out. Do not use an eraser.

There are 10 parts to this activity.

The activity

1. In row a, write an addition sign next to each calculation.

2. Now answer all the calculations in row a.

3. In row b, write a subtraction sign next to each calculation.

4. Now answer all the calculations in row b.

5. In row c, we are going to make a pattern of addition and subtraction calculations. Next to the first calculation, write an addition sign. Next to the second calculation, write a subtraction sign. Next to the third calculation, write an addition sign. Finish the pattern.

6. Now answer all the calculations in row c.

7. In row d, we are going to make another pattern of addition and subtraction calculations. Next to the first calculation, write a subtraction sign. Next to the second calculation, write an addition sign. Next to the third calculation, write a subtraction sign. Finish the pattern.

8. Now answer all the calculations in row d.

9. In each row draw a ring around the calculation with the largest answer.

10. Look at the answers to all of the calculations. Write your name under the smallest answer.

Answers

Discussion questions

↓ Under which answer did you write your name? (55)

↓ Read out a calculation you know the answer to.

■ What are the answers to all the calculations in the third row? (543, 269, 932, 137, 1045)

■ What were the numbers you drew a ring around? (743, 458, 1045, 784)

↑ Look at the last question in row c. What is the answer? (1045) How did you work it out? Did anyone work it out a different way?

↑ Which calculations did you answer incorrectly? What is the correct answer? Do you know how to work it out now? Will you know how to answer a question similar to this next time?

Activity 19

■ Develop and use written methods to record, support or explain
addition and subtraction of two-digit and three-digit numbers.

Date _____

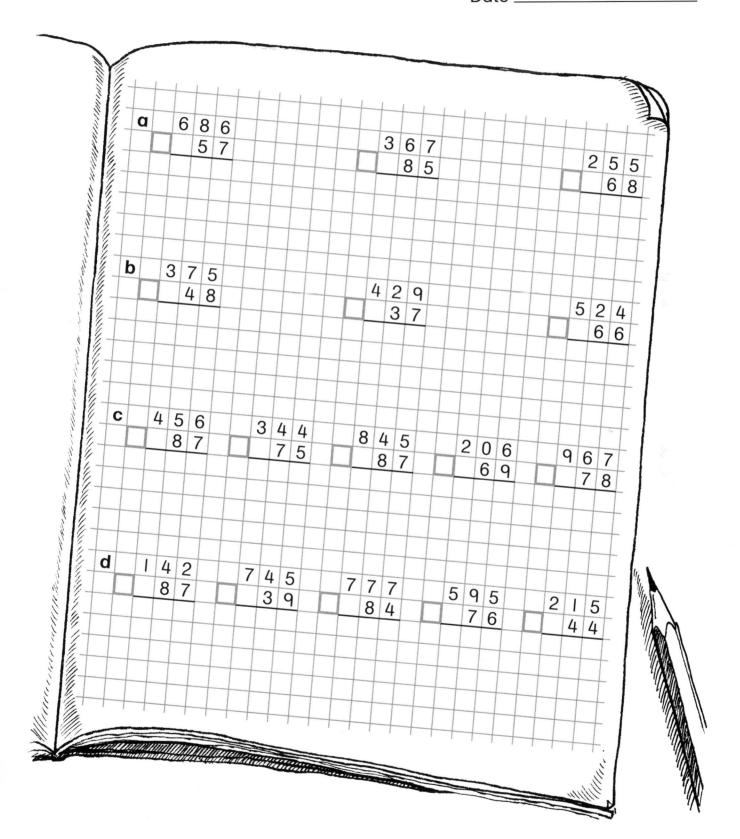

a.
- 686
- 57

- 367
- 85

- 255
- 68

b.
- 375
- 48

- 429
- 37

- 524
- 66

c.
- 456
- 87

- 344
- 75

- 845
- 87

- 206
- 69

- 967
- 78

d.
- 142
- 87

- 745
- 39

- 777
- 84

- 595
- 76

- 215
- 44

Year 3 Calculating

■ Use practical and informal written methods to multiply two-digit numbers.

Resources

Provide each child with the following:

■ a copy of Activity 20 pupil sheet
■ a pencil
■ a coloured pencil

Key words

zero, one, two…ten   ten, twenty, thirty…one hundred   one hundred, two hundred, three hundred…nine hundred   times   multiplied by   product   groups of   lots of

Say to the children:

Listen carefully.

I am going to tell you some things to do.

I will say them only once, so listen very carefully.

Do only the things you are told to do and nothing else.

If you make a mistake, cross it out. Do not use an eraser.

There are 13 parts to this activity.

The activity

1. Look at the calculations on the stapler. The number needed to complete one of the calculations is nine. Colour the box on that calculation.

2. Look at the calculations on the stapler again. The number needed to complete one of the calculations is 10. Write the number 10 in the box on that calculation.

3. Look at the calculations on the eraser. The number needed to complete one of the calculations is fifty. Write your name above that calculation.

4. Look at the calculations on the eraser again. The number needed to complete two of the calculations is 30. Write the number 30 in the boxes on those calculations.

5. Look at the calculations on the crayon. The number needed to complete one of the calculations is four. Write the number four in the box on that calculation.

6. Look at the calculations on the crayon again. The number needed to complete two of the calculations is 40. Colour the boxes on those calculations.

7. Look at the calculations on the sharpener. The number needed to complete two of the calculations is 60. Colour the boxes on those calculations.

8. Look at the calculations on the sharpener again. The number needed to complete two of the calculations is 100. Write the number 100 in the boxes on those calculations.

9. Look at the calculations on the ruler. The number needed to complete two of the calculations is 40. Colour the boxes on those calculations.

10. Look at the calculations on the ruler again. The number needed to complete three of the calculations is 20. Write the number 20 in the boxes on those calculations.

11. Look at the calculations on the pencil. The number needed to complete two of the calculations is three. Colour the boxes on those calculations.

12. Look at the calculations on the pencil again. The number needed to complete two of the calculations is 23. Write the number 23 in the boxes on those calculations.

13. Look at the calculations on the pencil again. The number needed to complete two of the calculations is 48. Draw a cross through the boxes on those calculations.

Answers

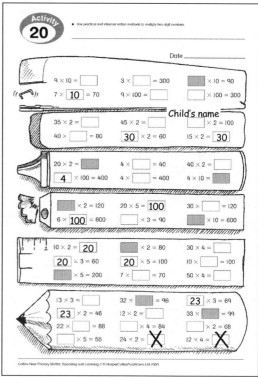

Discussion questions

↓ Look at the calculations on the eraser. What number did you write on two of those calculations? (30) What are those calculations? ($30 \times 2 = 60$ and $15 \times 2 = 30$)

↓ Find a calculation on the sheet that you know the answer to. What is it?

■ On which calculations did you draw a cross in the box? (24×2 and 12×4) What are the answers? (48)

■ Which calculations did you find easy/hard to answer? Why?

↑ Look at all the calculations where the box is coloured. Starting from the top of the sheet who can read all of these calculations including the missing numbers?

↑ Find a calculation on the sheet that you have not written an answer for. Read out that calculation and tell me the answer.

Activity 20

■ Use practical and informal written methods to multiply two-digit numbers.

Date _____

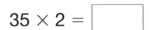

$9 \times 10 = \boxed{}$ $3 \times \boxed{} = 300$ $\boxed{} \times 10 = 90$

$7 \times \boxed{} = 70$ $9 \times 100 = \boxed{}$ $\boxed{} \times 100 = 300$

$35 \times 2 = \boxed{}$ $45 \times 2 = \boxed{}$ $\boxed{} \times 2 = 100$

$40 \times \boxed{} = 80$ $\boxed{} \times 2 = 60$ $15 \times 2 = \boxed{}$

$20 \times 2 = \boxed{}$ $4 \times \boxed{} = 40$ $40 \times 2 = \boxed{}$

$\boxed{} \times 100 = 400$ $4 \times \boxed{} = 400$ $4 \times 10 = \boxed{}$

$\boxed{} \times 2 = 120$ $20 \times 5 = \boxed{}$ $30 \times \boxed{} = 120$

$6 \times \boxed{} = 600$ $\boxed{} \times 3 = 90$ $\boxed{} \times 10 = 600$

$10 \times 2 = \boxed{}$ $\boxed{} \times 2 = 80$ $30 \times 4 = \boxed{}$

$\boxed{} \times 3 = 60$ $\boxed{} \times 5 = 100$ $10 \times \boxed{} = 100$

$\boxed{} \times 5 = 200$ $7 \times \boxed{} = 70$ $50 \times 4 = \boxed{}$

$13 \times 3 = \boxed{}$ $32 \times \boxed{} = 96$ $\boxed{} \times 3 = 69$

$\boxed{} \times 2 = 46$ $12 \times 2 = \boxed{}$ $33 \times \boxed{} = 99$

$22 \times \boxed{} = 88$ $\boxed{} \times 4 = 84$ $\boxed{} \times 2 = 68$

$\boxed{} \times 5 = 55$ $24 \times 2 = \boxed{}$ $12 \times 4 = \boxed{}$

Year 3 Calculating

- Use practical and informal written methods to divide two-digit numbers.
- (Divide multiples of 10 and 100 by 2, 10 or 100.)

Resources

Provide each child with the following:
- a copy of Activity 21 pupil sheet
- a red, blue, green and yellow coloured pencil

Key words

zero, one, two…ten   ten, twenty, thirty…one hundred   one hundred, two hundred, three hundred…nine hundred   divided by   one tenth   one hundredth

Say to the children:

Listen carefully.

I am going to tell you some things to do.

I will say them only once, so listen very carefully.

Do only the things you are told to do and nothing else.

If you make a mistake, cross it out. Do not use an eraser.

There are 13 parts to this activity.

The activity

1. What is 200 divided by 10? Find that number and colour it red.

2. What is 800 divided by 100? Find that number and colour it red.

3. What is 20 divided by two? Find that number and colour it red.

4. What is 400 divided by 100? Find that number and colour it blue.

5. What is 50 divided by two? Find that number and colour it blue.

6. What is 700 divided by 10? Find that number and colour it blue.

7. What is one hundredth of 600? Find that number and colour it green.

8. What is 90 divided by two? Find that number and colour it green.

9. What is one tenth of 500? Find that number and colour it green.

10. What is 70 divided by two? Find that number and colour it yellow.

11. What is one tenth of 900? Find that number and colour it yellow.

12. What is 300 divided by 100? Find that number and colour it yellow.

13. What is 80 divided by two? Find that number and write your name beside it.

Answers

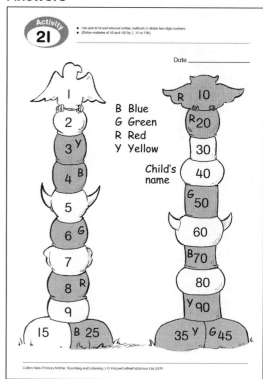

Discussion questions

↓ Which numbers did you colour green? (6, 45 and 50)

↓ What did you do to the number 70? (coloured it blue)

■ What is 800 divided by 10? (80) What is 800 divided by 100? (8)

■ 15 is half of what number? (30)

↑ What is another way of saying divided by 10/divided by 100? (one tenth/one hundredth)

↑ What is one tenth of 6000? (600) What is one hundredth of 6000? (60)

- Use practical and informal written methods to divide two-digit numbers.
- (Divide multiples of 10 and 100 by 2, 10 or 100.)

Date _____

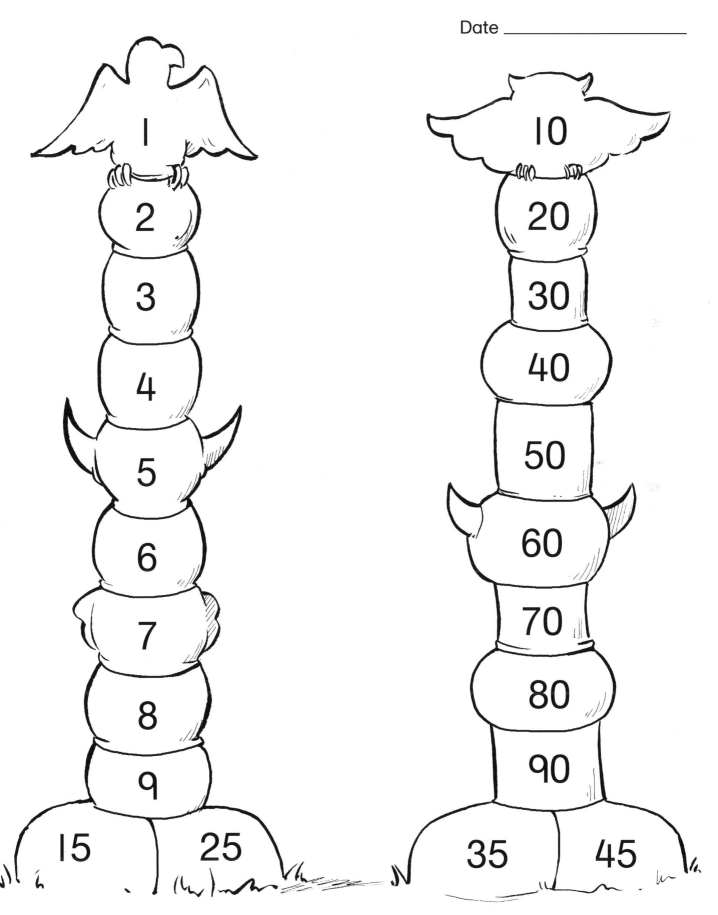

- Use practical and informal written methods to multiply and divide two-digit numbers.
- Multiply one-digit and two-digit numbers by 10 or 100, and describe the effect.
- (Divide multiples of 10 and 100 by 2, 10 or 100.)

Resources

Provide each child with the following:
- a copy of Activity 22 pupil sheet
- a pencil

Key words

zero, one, two…ten   ten, twenty, thirty…one hundred
one hundred, two hundred, three hundred…nine hundred
multiplication   times   multiplied by   product   groups of   lots of
division   divided by   one tenth   one hundredth   sign

Say to the children:

Listen carefully.

I am going to tell you some things to do.

I will say them only once, so listen very carefully.

Do only the things you are told to do and nothing else.

If you make a mistake, cross it out. Do not use an eraser.

There are 15 parts to this activity.

The activity

1. Look at table a. In the first grey box write one, in the second grey box write 10 and in the third box write 100.

2. Now fill in the boxes to complete table a.

3. Look at table b. In the first grey box write 10. In the second grey box write 100.

4. Now fill in the boxes to complete table b.

5. Look at circle c. In the grey circle write the multiplication sign followed by the number two.

6. Now fill in the answers to complete circle c.

7. Look at circle d. In the grey circle write the division sign followed by the number two.

8. Now fill in the answers to complete circle d.

9. Look at circle e. In the grey circle write the multiplication sign followed by the number three.

10. Now fill in the answers to complete circle e.

11. Look at circle f. In the grey circle write the multiplication sign followed by the number four.

12. Now fill in the answers to complete circle f.

13. Look at table g. In the first grey box write two, in the second grey box write three, in the third grey box write four, in the fourth grey box write five and in the fifth grey box write 10.

14. Now fill in the boxes to complete table g.

15. Write your name on the top of the sheet.

Answers

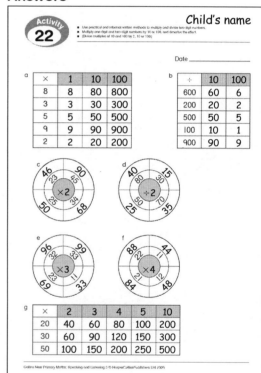

Discussion questions

⬇ Look at table a. What numbers did you write in the grey boxes? (1, 10 and 100) Choose any row in table a and tell me the answers.

⬇ Look at table a. What do you notice about the answers? (For each row, every answer is ten times the previous one.)
Look at table b. What do you notice about the answers? (For each row, every answer is one tenth of the previous one.)

■ What are the answers to circle d? (40, 15, 35, 25)

■ Did you make any errors? Which ones? Do you know what the correct answer is? How did you work it out?

⬆ Look at table g. Choose a row and call out the answers in it. What do you notice about the answers?

⬆ Which table or circle did you find the most difficult? Why do you think this might be?

- Use practical and informal written methods to multiply and divide two-digit numbers.
- Multiply one-digit and two-digit numbers by 10 or 100, and describe the effect.
- (Divide multiples of 10 and 100 by 2, 10 or 100.)

Date _____

a

×			
8			
3			
5			
9			
2			

b

÷		
600		
200		
500		
100		
900		

c

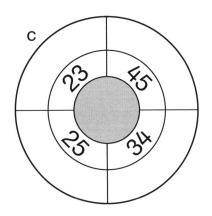

d

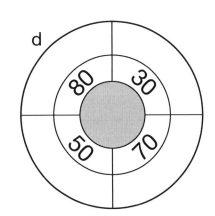

e

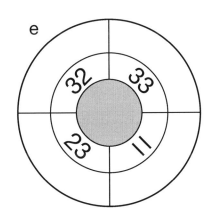

f

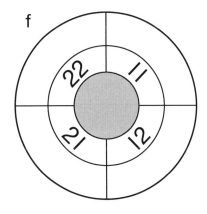

g

×					
20					
30					
50					

Year 3 Calculating

■ Find unit fractions of numbers and quantities, e.g. $\frac{1}{2}$, $\frac{1}{3}$, $\frac{1}{4}$ and $\frac{1}{6}$ of 12 litres.

Resources

Provide each child with the following:
■ a copy of Activity 23 pupil sheet ■ a pencil

Key words

one, two, three…ten fraction divided half/one half/halve
one third, one quarter, one fifth, one sixth, one seventh, one eighth,
one ninth, one tenth

Say to the children:

Listen carefully.

I am going to tell you some things to do.

I will say them only once, so listen very carefully.

Do only the things you are told to do and nothing else.

If you make a mistake, cross it out. Do not use an eraser.

There are 15 parts to this activity.

The activity

1. Look at the alphabet soup. Count all the 'U's. How many are there? Write this number in the star.

2. What is one seventh of the number in the star? Write the answer in the grey box.

3. Look at the alphabet soup again. Count all the 'I's. How many are there? Write this number in the rectangle.

4. What is one fifth of the number in the rectangle? Write the answer in the grey box.

5. Count all the 'A's. How many are there? Write this number in each of the squares.

6. What is a half of the number in the square? Write the answer in the grey box.

7. What is one eighth of the number in the square? Write the answer in the grey box.

8. Count all the 'O's. How many are there? Write this number in each of the circles.

9. What is one tenth of the number in the circle? Write the answer in the grey box.

10. What is one quarter of the number in the circle? Write the answer in the grey box.

11. Count all the 'E's. How many are there? Write this number in each of the triangles.

12. What is one third of the number in the triangle? Write the answer in the grey box.

13. What is one ninth of the number in the triangle? Write the answer in the grey box.

14. What is one sixth of the number in the triangle? Write the answer in the grey box.

15. Look at all the numbers in the grey boxes. Write your name under the largest number.

Answers

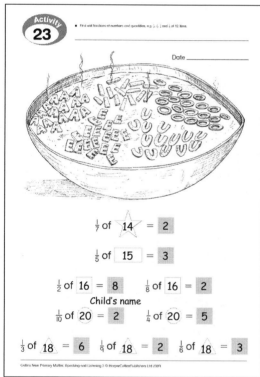

Discussion questions

↓ What number did you write in the squares? (16) What is a half of 16? (8)

↓ How many 'O's are in the alphabet soup? (20) What is one tenth of 20? (2)

■ What is one seventh of 14? (2)

■ What is one third/one sixth/one ninth of 18? (6/3/2) What do you notice?

↑ How many 'A's and 'U's are in the soup altogether? (30) What is one tenth/one fifth of 30? (3/6)

↑ What is one fifth of 15? (3) What are two fifths of 15? (6) What are three fifths of 15? (9) How did you work this out?

■ Find unit fractions of numbers and quantities, e.g. $\frac{1}{2}$, $\frac{1}{3}$, $\frac{1}{4}$ and $\frac{1}{6}$ of 12 litres.

Date _____

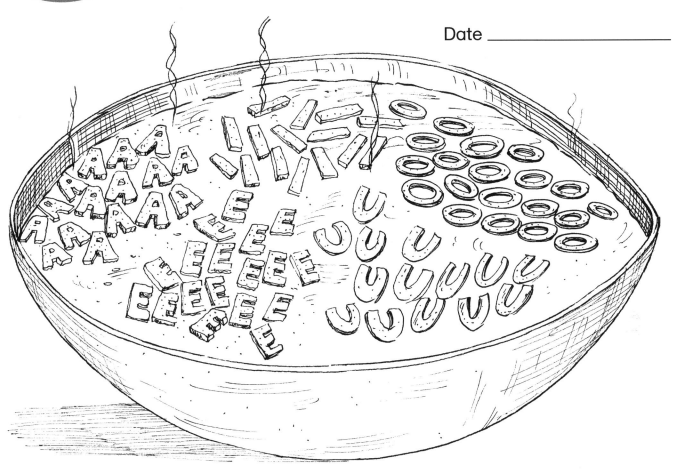

$\frac{1}{7}$ of ☆ = ▢

$\frac{1}{5}$ of ▭ = ▢

$\frac{1}{2}$ of ▢ = ▢ $\frac{1}{8}$ of ▢ = ▢

$\frac{1}{10}$ of ◯ = ▢ $\frac{1}{4}$ of ◯ = ▢

$\frac{1}{3}$ of △ = ▢ $\frac{1}{9}$ of △ = ▢ $\frac{1}{6}$ of △ = ▢

■ Relate 2-D shapes and 3-D solids to drawings of them;
describe, visualise, classify the shapes.

Resources

Provide each child with the following:

■ a copy of Activity 24 pupil sheet
■ a red, blue, green, yellow, orange and purple coloured pencil

Key words

3-D shapes   cube   cuboid   pyramid   sphere   hemisphere
cone   cylinder   2-D shapes   square   rectangle   triangle
circle   pentagon   hexagon   octagon

Say to the children:

Listen carefully.

I am going to tell you some things to do.

I will say them only once, so listen very carefully.

Do only the things you are told to do and nothing else.

If you make a mistake, cross it out. Do not use an eraser.

There are 15 parts to this activity.

The activity

1. Look at all the shapes on the sheet. Find all the squares and colour them red.

2. Find all the cuboids and colour them blue.

3. Find all the pyramids and colour them green.

4. Find all the circles and colour them yellow.

5. Find all the hemispheres and colour them orange.

6. Find all the hexagons and colour them purple.

7. Find all the octagons and write your name inside each of these shapes.

8. Find all the cubes and colour them red.

9. Find all the rectangles and colour them blue.

10. Find all the triangles and colour them green.

11. Find all the spheres and colour them purple.

12. Find all the pentagons and colour them orange.

13. Find all the cones and colour them yellow.

14. Look at all the shapes you have not coloured. What do we call these shapes? Inside each shape, write the name of the shape.

15. Look at all the shapes on the sheet. Which of these shapes are quadrilaterals? Write the letter Q inside each of the quadrilaterals.

Answers

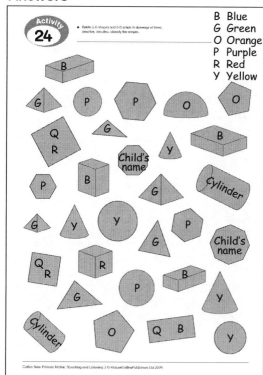

Discussion questions

↓ Which shapes did you colour red? (squares and cubes)

↓ Choose a shape on the sheet and name it. Is this shape a 3-D or 2-D shape?

■ Which shape did you not colour? (cylinder) How many cylinders are there on the sheet? (2)

■ How many shapes are on the sheet? (31) How many of these are 3-D/2-D shapes? (16/15)

↑ Look at all the shapes on the sheet. How many quadrilaterals/prisms are there? (3/5) What do we call these shapes? (squares and rectangles/cubes and cuboids)

↑ Choose a shape on the sheet. Name it and tell me some of its properties.

Activity 24

■ Relate 2-D shapes and 3-D solids to drawings of them;
describe, visualise, classify the shapes.

Date _____

■ Read and record the vocabulary of position, direction and movement.

Resources

Provide each child with the following:
■ a copy of Activity 25 pupil sheet
■ a coloured pencil

Key words

position square grid row column left right

Say to the children:

Listen carefully.

I am going to tell you some things to do.

I will say them only once, so listen very carefully.

Do only the things you are told to do and nothing else.

If you make a mistake, cross it out. Do not use an eraser.

There are 21 parts to this activity.

The activity

1. Colour square C 2.

2. Colour square D 8.

3. Colour square J 1.

4. Colour square B 6.

5. Colour square D 4.

6. Colour square I 2.

7. Colour square D 5.

8. Colour square C 7.

9. Colour square J 2.

10. Colour square C 1.

11. Colour square J 6.

12. Colour square D 3.

13. Colour square D 7.

14. Colour square C 3.

15. Colour square E 8.

16. Colour square J 4.

17. Colour square D 6.

18. Colour square B 7.

19. Colour square I 1.

20. Colour square C 6.

21. Write your name to the right of the object you have just drawn.

Answers

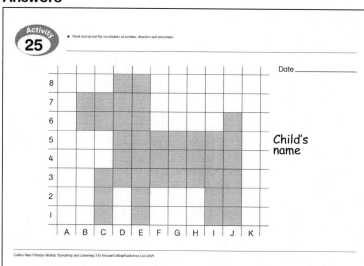

Discussion questions

↓ What have you just drawn? (dog)

↓ When did you realise you were drawing a dog?

■ Which square is the dog's tail? (J 6)

■ Where did you write your name? (to the right of the dog)

↑ Tell me a square that was already coloured. (E 1, E 2, E 3, E 4, E 5, E 6, E 7, F 3, F 4, F 5, G 3, G 4, G 5, H 3, H 4, H 5, I 3, I 4, I 5, J 3 and J 5)

↑ In column C which rows did you colour? (1, 2, 3, 6 and 7)

■ Read and record the vocabulary of position, direction and movement.

Date _____

	A	B	C	D	E	F	G	H	I	J	K
8											
7											
6											
5											
4											
3											
2											
1											

Year 3 Measuring

- Solve one-step and two-step problems involving measures (length).
- Read, to the nearest division and half-division, scales that are numbered or partially numbered.

Resources

Provide each child with the following:
- a copy of Activity 26 pupil sheet
- a pencil

Key words

centimetre   metre   short/shorter/shortest   tall/taller/tallest
more   difference

Say to the children:

Listen carefully.

I am going to tell you some things to do.

I will say them only once, so listen very carefully.

Do only the things you are told to do and nothing else.

If you make a mistake, cross it out. Do not use an eraser.

There are 12 parts to this activity.

The activity

1. How tall is flower a? Write the answer on flowerpot one at the bottom of the sheet.

2. How tall is flower b? Write the answer on flowerpot two.

3. How tall is flower d? Write the answer on flowerpot three.

4. How tall is flower c? Write the answer on flowerpot four.

5. How many more centimetres will flower a need to grow to reach one metre? Write the answer on flowerpot five.

6. How many more centimetres will flower d need to grow to reach one metre? Write the answer on flowerpot six.

7. How many more centimetres will flower b need to grow to reach one metre? Write the answer on flowerpot seven.

8. How many more centimetres will flower c need to grow to reach one metre? Write the answer on flowerpot eight.

9. How much taller is flower a than flower d? Write the answer on flowerpot nine.

10. How much shorter is flower b than flower d? Write the answer on flowerpot ten.

11. What is the difference in height between the tallest and the shortest flowers? Write the answer on flowerpot twelve.

12. Write your name on flowerpot eleven.

Answers

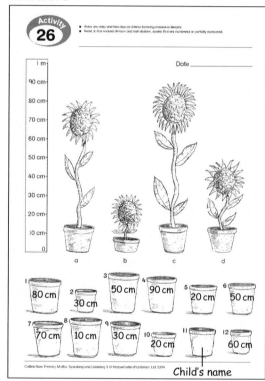

Discussion questions

↓ How tall is flower c? (90 cm)

↓ Where did you write your name? (flowerpot eleven)

■ How many more centimetres will flower d need to grow to reach one metre? (50 cm)

■ How much taller is flower a than flower d? (30 cm)

↑ What is the difference in height between the tallest and the shortest flowers? (60 cm)

↑ If you were to stand flowers a and d on top of each other how high would they be? (130 cm) How tall is that in metres and centimetres? (1 m 30 cm)

- Solve one-step and two-step problems involving measures (length).
- Read, to the nearest division and half-division, scales that are numbered or partially numbered.

Date _____

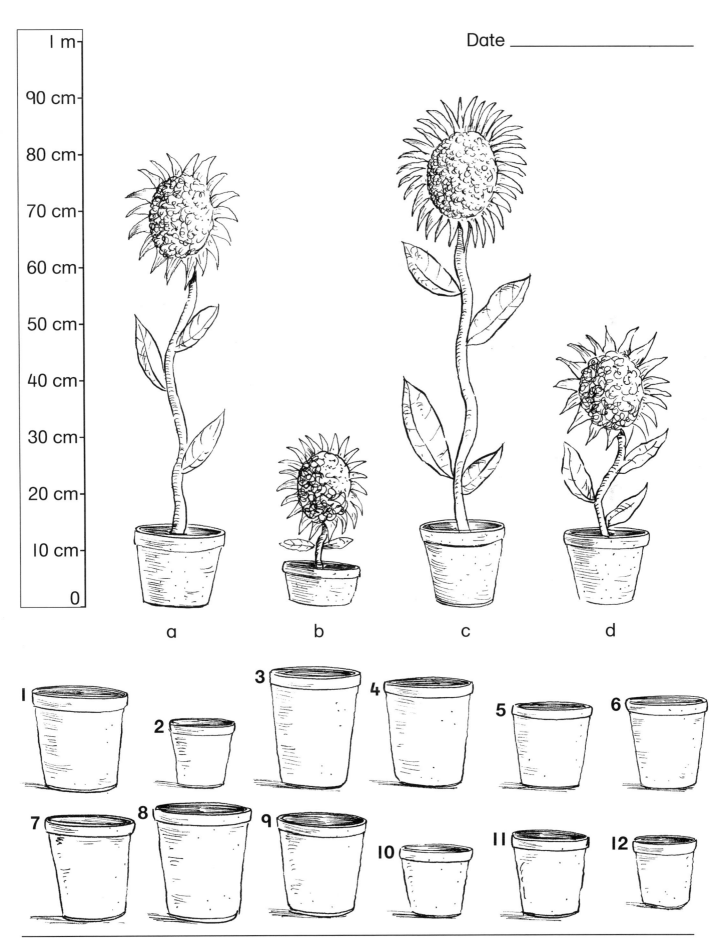

a　　　　　b　　　　　　c　　　　　　d

1　2　3　4　5　6

7　8　9　10　11　12

Year 3 Measuring

- Solve one-step and two-step problems involving measures (mass).
- Read, to the nearest division and half-division, scales that are numbered or partially numbered.

Resources

Provide each child with the following:
- a copy of Activity 27 pupil sheet
- a pencil

Key words

zero, one, two…ten   weigh   weight   kilograms   grams
difference   heavy/heavier/heaviest   light/lighter/lightest   most
least   approximately

Say to the children:

Listen carefully.

I am going to tell you some things to do.

I will say them only once, so listen very carefully.

Do only the things you are told to do and nothing else.

If you make a mistake, cross it out. Do not use an eraser.

There are 12 parts to this activity.

The activity

1. Sarah, Lee, Michael and David went strawberry-picking. What was the weight of the strawberries that Sarah picked, to the nearest half kilogram? Write the answer on strawberry one.

2. What was the weight of the strawberries that Lee picked, to the nearest half kilogram? Write the answer on strawberry two.

3. What was the weight of the strawberries that Michael picked, to the nearest half kilogram? Write the answer on strawberry four.

4. What was the weight of the strawberries that David picked, to the nearest kilogram? Write the answer on strawberry three.

5. Whose strawberries were the heaviest? Write their name on strawberry five.

6. Whose strawberries weighed least? Write their name on strawberry six.

7. What is the total weight of the strawberries Michael and David picked, to the nearest half kilogram? Write the answer on strawberry eight.

8. What is the total weight of the strawberries Michael and Sarah picked? Write the answer on strawberry seven.

9. Write your name on strawberry nine.

10. What is the difference in weight between the strawberries Sarah and Lee picked? Write the answer on strawberry ten.

11. What is the difference in weight between the strawberries David and Lee picked? Write the answer on strawberry twelve.

12. When Lee took his strawberries home, his family ate three kilograms. What is the weight of the strawberries that are left? Write the answer on strawberry eleven.

Answers

Discussion questions

↓ Whose strawberries weighed the most? (Lee's)

↓ What was the weight of the strawberries that Michael picked, to the nearest half kilogram? ($3\frac{1}{2}$ kg) Where did you write the answer? (strawberry 4)

■ Approximately what is the difference in weight between the strawberries Sarah and Lee picked? (2 kg)

■ Put the weights of the strawberries in order starting with the lightest. (2 kg, $3\frac{1}{2}$ kg, $4\frac{1}{2}$ kg, $6\frac{1}{2}$ kg)

↑ Approximately what is the total weight of all the strawberries picked? ($16\frac{1}{2}$ kg)

↑ If strawberries cost £2 a kilogram to pick, approximately how much did Sarah/Lee/Michael/David have to pay for the strawberries? (£9/£13/£7/£4)

■ Solve one-step and two-step problems involving measures (mass).
■ Read, to the nearest division and half-division, scales that are numbered or partially numbered.

Date _____

- Solve one-step and two-step problems involving measures (capacity).
- Read, to the nearest division and half-division, scales that are numbered or partially numbered.

Resources

Provide each child with the following:
- a copy of Activity 28 pupil sheet
- a pencil

Key words

zero, one, two…one hundred   capacity   fill   full   half full
empty   litre   half litre   how many?

Say to the children:

Listen carefully.

I am going to tell you some things to do.

I will say them only once, so listen very carefully.

Do only the things you are told to do and nothing else.

If you make a mistake, cross it out. Do not use an eraser.

There are 12 parts to this activity.

The activity

Questions one to six refer to the objects at the top of the sheet.

1. Look at the bucket, bottle and glass. Draw a ring around the object you think has a capacity of about two litres.
2. Look at the jug, cup and fish tank. Draw a ring around the object you think has a capacity of about one litre.
3. Look at the dustbin, mug and teapot. Draw a ring around the object you think has a capacity of about 80 litres.
4. How many millilitres are there in one litre? Write the answer under the teapot.
5. Look at the bath tub, carton of milk and watering can. Draw a ring around the object you think has a capacity of about 10 litres.
6. Write your name above the bath tub.

Questions seven to twelve refer to the objects at the bottom of the sheet.

7. Look at the bucket and the dustbin. The bucket holds eight litres of water and the dustbin holds 80 litres of water. How many buckets of water are needed to fill the dustbin? Write the answer above the bucket.
8. How many millilitres are there in half a litre? Write the answer under the bucket.
9. Look at the jug and the glass. The jug holds three litres of squash. How many times will it fill a half litre glass? Write the answer on the jug.
10. Look at the measuring jug and the saucepan. The measuring jug holds two litres of water and the saucepan holds 10 litres of water. How many jugs of water are needed to fill the saucepan? Write the answer under the saucepan.
11. Look at the fish tank. The fish tank holds 16 litres of water. At the moment it is exactly half full. How many more litres will fill the fish tank? Write the answer on the fish tank.
12. Look at the jug and six glasses. If the jug holds two litres, how many half litre glasses can be filled from the jug? Colour that number of glasses.

Answers

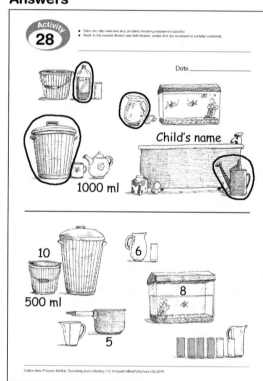

Discussion questions

↓ How many millilitres are there in one litre/half a litre? (1000 ml/500 ml)

↓ Look at the bucket, bottle and glass at the top of the sheet. Which container did you draw a ring around? (bottle)

■ Look at the jug and the glass at the bottom of the sheet. If the jug holds three litres of squash, how many times will it fill a half litre glass? (6)

■ Look at the fish tank. If the tank holds 16 litres of water and it is only half full, how many more litres are needed to fill the tank? (8 litres) How many millilitres is this? (8000 ml)

↑ How many millilitres are there in two/three and a half/five/seven and a half litres? (2000 ml/3500 ml/5000 ml/7500 ml)

↑ Look at the jug and six glasses at the bottom of the sheet. If each glass holds half a litre, how many millilitres are needed to fill three/four glasses? (1500 ml/2000 ml)

Activity 28

- Solve one-step and two-step problems involving measures (capacity).
- Read, to the nearest division and half-division, scales that are numbered or partially numbered.

Date _____

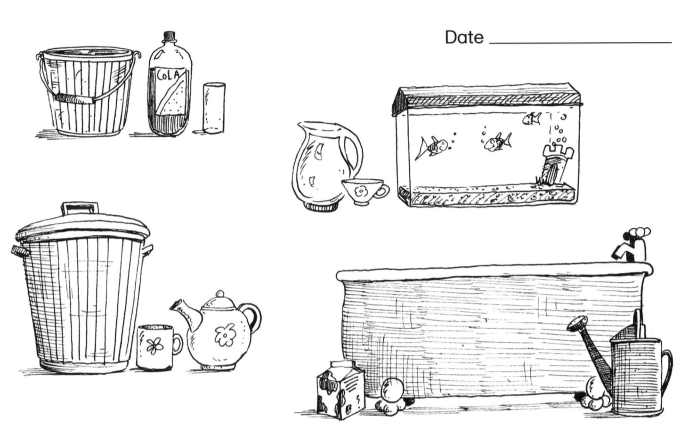

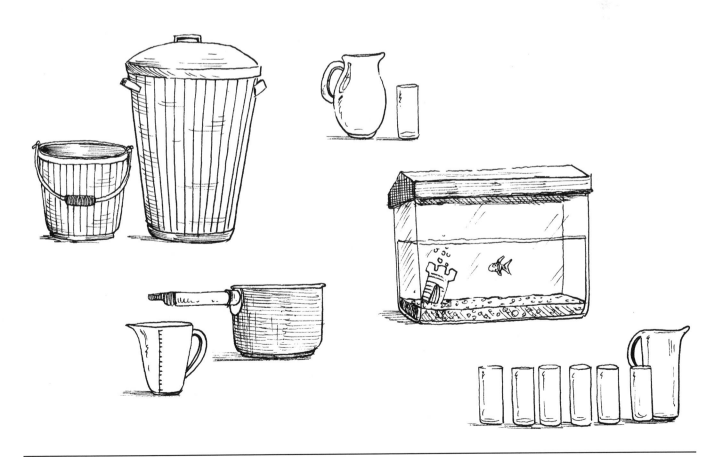

■ Read the time on a 12-hour digital clock and to the nearest five minutes on an analogue clock.

Resources

Provide each child with the following:
■ a copy of Activity 29 pupil sheet   ■ a pencil
■ a red, blue, green and yellow coloured pencil

Key words

one, two, three…twelve   five, ten, fifteen…sixty   o'clock   clock
time   minute   past   to   analogue   digital

Say to the children:

Listen carefully.

I am going to tell you some things to do.

I will say them only once, so listen very carefully.

Do only the things you are told to do and nothing else.

If you make a mistake, cross it out. Do not use an eraser.

There are 15 parts to this activity.

The activity

1. Find the clock that reads seven twenty-five. Write seven twenty-five under that clock in digital notation.

2. Find the clock that reads quarter to twelve. Colour that clock red.

3. Find clock c. Make the clock read two twenty.

4. Find clock g. Make the clock read seven fifty.

5. Find the clock that reads one forty. Write one forty under that clock in digital notation.

6. Find the clock that reads nine fifteen. Colour that clock blue.

7. Find clock i. Make the clock read five minutes past four.

8. Find clock l. Make the clock read twenty-five minutes to three.

9. Find the clock that reads five to seven. Colour that clock green.

10. Find the clock that reads ten past four. Write your name under that clock.

11. Find clock d. Make the clock read half past twelve.

12. Find clock n. Make the clock read ten past eleven.

13. Find the clock that reads seven forty-five. Colour that clock yellow.

14. Find clock j. Make the clock read five o'clock.

15. Find clock a. Make the clock read quarter past four.

Answers

Discussion questions

↓ What did you do to clock m? (coloured it yellow) What time does the clock read? (quarter to eight)

↓ Which clock shows the time of five minutes past four? (clock i)

■ Look at the clock you coloured blue. What time does it read? (9:15) What is another way of saying that time? (quarter past nine)

■ Look at clocks i and o. What do you notice about these times? (five minutes apart)

↑ Look at clock l. What time does it read? (twenty five to three) What will the clock read in fifteen minutes' time? (ten to three)

↑ Look at clock f. What time have you written under the clock? (1:40) What is another way of saying this time? (twenty to two)

■ Read the time on a 12-hour digital clock and to the nearest five minutes on an analogue clock.

Date _____

Year 3 Handling data

■ Answer a question by collecting, organising and interpreting data; use tally charts, frequency tables, and bar charts to represent results and illustrate observations.

Resources

Provide each child with the following:
■ a copy of Activity 30 pupil sheet
■ a coloured pencil

You will also need 40 randomly selected playing cards, shuffled and placed face down in a pile.

Key words

tally   tally mark   frequency table   bar chart   intervals
horizontal   vertical   suit   hearts   diamonds   clubs   spades

Say to the children:

Listen carefully.

I am going to tell you some things to do.

I will say them only once, so listen very carefully.

Do only the things you are told to do and nothing else.

If you make a mistake, cross it out. Do not use an eraser.

There are 6 parts to this activity.

The activity

1. Write your name above the date.

2. This activity is about collecting and organising data in simple frequency tables and bar charts.

    I am going to choose a card and call out the suit.

    Each time I call out the suit you have to make a tally mark on the frequency table.

    (Choose a card and call out the suit. Continue until all forty cards have been chosen.)

3. Look at all the tally marks. Count them up and complete the frequency table.

4. Look at the bar chart. Zero is already written at the bottom of the vertical axis. Look back at the frequency table and decide on the interval you need along the vertical axis.

5. Complete the vertical axis on the bar chart.

6. Now use the information in the frequency table to complete the bar chart.

Answers

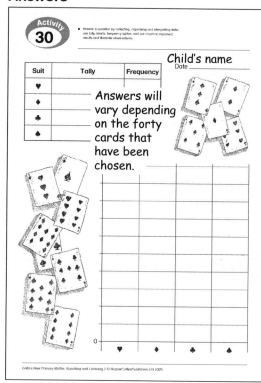

Discussion questions

↓ How many of the cards chosen were hearts?

↓ Which suit was chosen the most?

■ There were *x* cards of one suit chosen. Which suit was that?

■ Altogether how many cards did I choose? (40)

↑ How many of the cards chosen were clubs and diamonds?

↑ Were there more hearts or clubs? How many more?

■ Answer a question by collecting, organising and interpreting data; use tally charts, frequency tables, and bar charts to represent results and illustrate observations.

Date _____

Suit	Tally	Frequency
♥		
♦		
♣		
♠		

♥	♦	♣	♠

0